Risk the Journey

Answering God's Call to Proclaim His Word

Bill J. Leonard

Woman's Missionary Union, SBC
Birmingham, Alabama

Woman's Missionary Union
P. O. Box 830010
Birmingham, AL 35283-0010

© 1995 by Woman's Missionary Union

All rights reserved. First printing 1995
Printed in the United States of America

Dewey Decimal Classification: 248.4
Subject Headings: CHRISTIAN LIFE
                     MISSIONS
                     CHURCH—BIBLICAL TEACHING

Cover photograph by Dan Bryan.

ISBN: 1-56309-122-4
W953102•0595•15M1

To my parents
Marvin R. Leonard
and
Lavelle Henton Leonard
with gratitude

CONTENTS

PREFACE

Writing this book was a learning experience for me. First, research took me "back to the sources," to letters, diaries, journals, autobiographies, and other materials written by fascinating individuals. Some, like the autobiography of Peter Cartwright, the Methodist circuit rider, I have lived with for a long time. Others, like the memoir of Congregational missionary Harriet Winslow, were new to me. Each resource introduced me to the reality of Christian witness and mission as expressed in real human beings given to moments of courage and terror, selflessness and selfishness, but risking themselves for the sake of Christ's gospel. They were not without doubts, and they could not escape sickness, danger, and death, but they were willing to take a chance on God, grace, and eternity. Reading their stories, I was struck by their humanity and the faith they manifested, sometimes in the most difficult circumstances.

Second, I was reminded of the great diversity of the "saints" who make up the church of Christ. Some were aggressive and self-confident; others were shy and uncertain about their calling. Some left their homes and families and never looked back; others longed for home all the days of their lives. They affirmed the dogmas of various Christian traditions: Protestant, Catholic, Methodist, Baptist, Presbyterian, Congregational, and Pentecostal. Many thought that all other traditions were heretical; some accepted God's grace and truth wherever it was revealed to them. At their best, they looked beyond themselves to a higher calling which binds all God's people—faith in Christ and service in His name.

Third, I strongly believe that we, like those who have gone before us, must discover what it means to risk the journey of faith. Our times are no better or no worse than those of the people discussed in this brief volume. True enough, we confront different dangers and challenges, but we, like they, are called to risk something of ourselves for the sake of the gospel of Christ. As I write these words, a group of students from Samford University are departing for Indonesia to participate in a two-week mission project. Because of the benefits of jet travel, they will depart, offer their ministry, and return in less time than it took Lottie Moon to reach nineteenth-century China. Yet in a world where planes can crash, cars collide, and political unrest create unexpected violence, these students must risk something on the journey to Indonesia whether their stay is brief or lengthy. As we enter the twenty-first century, the Holy Spirit is still out there ahead of us, calling us to missions old and new, challenging us to take the good news to the poor, the broken, and the imprisoned—risky business.

Finally, on the threshold of a new century, we listen to the voices of the past to help us shape our identity in the present. The people whose lives and words are recounted here remind us that we have an identity, we belong to a people, we have a history which links us with those who went before us and encourages us to pass on a heritage and a hope to those who come after us. For our generation, the issue of identity is significant. As denominational identities decline or are redefined, we must give serious attention to the legacy we will pass on to a new generation of Christians. What does it mean to be Christian in the second millennium? What does it mean to be Baptist or Methodist, Catholic or Pentecostal? Do those traditions have value for the future? What do our forebearers teach us about our own identity as citizens of the kingdom of God? Does their vision inform our own? What timeless elements should we retain and promote to our children?

Through it all there is the wonder of God's good presence, offered to those who struggle in every age with the meaning of the gospel. Perhaps in listening to the stories of others we shall discover something of that gospel for ourselves. Good news.

Bill J. Leonard
Birmingham, Alabama 1995

Defining the Christian's Mission

Our first step was to consult a physician. Dr. L. visited me, and at once made himself so well acquainted with my case that I felt much confidence in him. He did not encourage any hope that I should soon be well; and advised us to proceed to Calcutta, or try a land journey. We waited some days, and no passage by ship could be secured. The rains had fully commenced. How then could we undertake a land journey? There was no alternative, and we made arrangements to go to Bangalore, two hundred miles distant, in palankeens. The rains continued so violent that we were detained a few days. When they abated, we prepared to leave. . . . The next morning a note came in, saying that a ship was approaching the town. This induced us to turn our faces again towards the sea. Some friends advised us not to venture out, as storms and a long passage were to be expected. We however sought and found direction. . . . We reached Calcutta Sabbath morning, the 27th [November 1825] the same day on which, as we afterwards learned, our darling [daughter] Harriet died at Jaffna. We did not go on shore till next morning."[1]

"But a few months ago my home was full, now so silent and lonely—Samuel, Noel, my precious wife, with Jesus; the

elder children far, far away . . . Often, of late years, has duty
called me from my loved ones, but I have returned, and so
warm has been the welcome! Now I am alone. Can it be that
there is no return from this journey, no home-gathering to
look forward to! Is it real, and not a sorrowful dream, that
those dearest to me lie beneath the cold sod? Ah, it is indeed
true! But not more so, than that there is a home-coming await-
ing me which no parting shall break into, no tears mar. . . .
Love gave the blow that for a little while makes the desert
more dreary, but heaven more home-like. 'I go to prepare a
place for you': and is not our part of the preparation the peo-
pling it with those we love?"²

"Here every native I meet is an enemy to me because I am
an Englishman. England appears almost a heaven upon earth,
because there one is not viewed as an unjust intruder. . . . The
thought of interrupting a crowd of busy people like those at
Patna, whose every day is a market day, with a message
about eternity, without command of language sufficient to
explain and defend myself, and so of becoming the scorn of
the rabble without doing them good, was offensive to my
pride. The manifest disaffection of the people, and the contempt with which they eyed me, confirmed my dread."³

These stories are missionary stories. They are narratives of
struggle, hurt, disappointment, and courage. This book
includes stories about missionaries. It explores the risk of the
gospel journey for those who travel far away and those who
remain at home. To suggest that the Christian life is a journey
or pilgrimage is to focus on the following issues: where the
gospel takes us, where we take the gospel, and what it means
to risk everything for Jesus and His way of living in the world.

To follow Christ is to embark on a journey. It is to set out
on a way of life that transforms and informs every facet of our
experience. It is to open the door to growth, change, and
rebirth, not simply in one spiritual event but in the journey of
a lifetime. Jesus said that to follow Him was to deny ourselves
and take up the cross (Matt. 16:24).

The Apostle Paul described the Christian experience in
terms that refer to a journey, even a race. He wrote to the

Philippians, "It is not to be thought that I have already achieved all this. I have not yet reached perfection, but I press on, hoping to take hold of that for which Christ once took hold of me. My friends, I do not reckon myself to have got hold of it yet. All I can say is this: forgetting what is behind me, and reaching out for that which lies ahead, I press towards the goal to win the prize which is God's call to the life above, in Christ Jesus" (Phil. 3:12-14 NEB).

To choose Christ and the gospel life, therefore, is to follow Christ, to press toward the prize, to journey along the way of the cross as God's people. This journey is an adventure as well as a responsibility. It is also a risk, since none of us can ever know what lies ahead. We are thus called to trust in God and follow. His command is to "go to all peoples everywhere and make them my disciples: Baptize them in the name of the Father, the Son, and the Holy Spirit, and teach them everything I have commanded you" (Matt 28: 19-20*a* TEV). This is the mission of all Christ's church.

This book, therefore, is also about the mission of the gospel for the church and the individual. The excerpts that introduce this chapter are taken from three nineteenth-century missionary journals. They are memoirs that acquaint us with the depth of spirit and struggle that is at the heart of the missionary endeavor. Throughout this book extensive attention will be given to the words of the missionaries themselves. Materials are taken from their journals, memoirs, letters, sermons, and other descriptions of their life and work. They reveal the wide diversity of personalities, backgrounds, influences, and approaches that characterize the lives of those involved in the church's great mission.

Some of the persons discussed and quoted here were sent out across America or around the world by missionary societies established for sending missionaries. They are part of a missionary community that long has sought to take the good news of Christ to the ends of the earth. They were chosen, funded (such as it was), and commissioned by various missionary societies and denominational boards charged with spreading the gospel around the world.

Other missionaries went on their own, not sent by a missions board or agency, but were no less called, whether confronting the American frontier or bound for Europe, Africa, or Asia. Many of these people simply went out alone in response to what they believed to be the call of Almighty God upon them. Some were preachers, and still others were teachers, physicians, or organizers. Other believers saw themselves as enablers, facilitating the missionary task while unable to participate directly in the missionary endeavor. Some remained at home; others went out. Some raised funds; others were funded. All gave themselves to prayer for God's guidance in whatever work they undertook. All were journeying in Christ's name. All discovered something of the risk of the gospel, and they passed it on to us through their written observations.

The risks they confronted were considerable. Many missionaries struggled with a sense of identity regarding the specifics of their Christian beliefs and their understanding of themselves in the total life of the Christian church. They did not always agree among themselves about the best way to express Christianity.

Likewise, they confronted the question of place—where they were, where they went, what they encountered, and the way in which location shaped the formation of Christian belief and practice. So, too, they were compelled to face the issue of community, both Christian and secular. They often had to learn to live in communities that were new, even "foreign" to their previous experience. They also had to learn to live with other people who were often quite different from themselves. Community, even Christian community—a genuine sense of belonging and acceptance—is not easily achieved. The quest for Christian life, life together, is a major challenge for those involved in Christ's mission.

Sometimes, however, community is not compatible with conscience; and risk invariably involves the risk of conscience. At such times, conscience may demand that men and women stand alone, facing a hostile majority for the sake of conviction. It is conscience that carried people into prison, exile, and even death for the gospel. The experiences of earlier generations of believers encourages us in our own struggles with conscience. The call to conscience, of course, reminds us that the missionary task also involves the risk of sacrifice.

Through the writings of the missionaries we discover the sacrifices they confronted in their willingness to tell the story of Jesus. Health, family, finances, and conflict were among those issues that brought the reality of sacrifice to generation after generation of missionaries. To serve in Christ's name was and is to face the reality of sacrifice. In the face of such sacrifice, spirituality—the life of prayer, study, worship, and contemplation—is essential. Through the life of the Spirit, those involved in missions find strength and courage to endure and persevere. The writings cited throughout this volume demonstrate the depth of communion with God the missionaries had in the midst of both success and failure. Yet growing spirituality itself is a risk, a "leap of faith," in God's continuing presence in even the most terrible moments of life.

Through it all there is the irony of missions, the presence of God in unexpected places, persons, and events. Irony reveals itself in God's choices for the missionary vocation—people who at times seem among the least likely candidates as ambassadors for God's kingdom. Likewise, God often reveals Himself in seemingly impossible circumstances; in what appears at times to be complete failure, the kingdom comes. Irony and its accompanying humor shape the missionary journey from start to finish. All of these elements—irony, community, identity, place, sacrifice, and conscience—help shape the church's understanding of the nature of the Christian mission. Each of these elements contains significant elements of risk.

Whatever their task, these missionary visionaries were ministers, doing specific kinds of Christian ministry wherever they found themselves. Some retained ministries that reflected the traditional approaches of their day. Others explored new possibilities. Almost all discovered that their sense of ministry was broadened by their participation in missionary causes.

But what, after all, is the nature of the Christian mission itself? What does it mean to be on mission in the world? The idea of the church's mission is the source of great discussion and sometimes debate. Therefore, definitions and qualifications are required from the beginning. What in the world is the meaning of the church's mission? In brief, the mission of the church begins with God as revealed in Jesus Christ. The mission of the church is to make known the good news of Jesus' life and teaching, His death and resurrection, and the impact of those truths in the world. William Owen Carver, the prominent Baptist missiologist, in the early part of this century called Christian missions "the extensive realization of God's redemptive purpose in Christ by means of human messengers." Carver was careful to affirm the missionary calling of all Christians, noting, "It is not possible closely to mark missions off from other work in that kingdom of God which it is ever the first duty of every disciple to seek. It will be suggestive to say that missions introduce the kingdom of heaven which other work deepens and develops in the extent and power of its influence in the whole life of man."[4]

Others who sought to describe the church's mission saw it as an imperative to communicate the gospel to all persons. Methodist layman John R. Mott (1865–1955) was one of the most significant spokespersons for the missionary cause in the modern era. Mott was a leader in efforts to unite all Christians in missions and ministry around the world. His response to the church's mission is evident in these passionate words: "Our sense of obligation must be intensified when we ask ourselves this question, If we do not preach Christ where He has not been named, who will? 'God has "committed unto us the word of reconciliation," and from whom shall the heathen now living ever hear that word, if the Christians of the present day fail to discharge the debt?' We know their need; we know the only remedy; we have access to them; we are able to go. . . . The Golden Rule by which we profess to live impels us to it. The example of Christ, who was moved with compassion to meet even the bodily hunger of the multitudes, should inspire us to go forth with the Word of life to the millions who are wandering in helplessness in the shadow of death."[5]

The mission of the church is to tell the story of Jesus and live that story to the fullest, wherever we may be. It is to recount that story to those who have never heard as well as to those who need to hear it again and again. It is also to bring that story, in all its implications, to bear on every aspect of human life.

And what is the story? At Pentecost, the Apostle Peter outlined it brilliantly when he declared to the people gathered in Jerusalem: "Jesus of Nazareth, a man attested to you by God with deeds of power, wonders, and signs that God did through him among you, as you yourselves know—this man, handed over to you according to the definite plan and foreknowledge of God, you crucified and killed by the hands of those outside the law. But God raised him up, having freed him from death, because it was impossible for him to be held in its power" (Acts 2:22*b*-24 NRSV).

Over 1,900 years later, Christians are still echoing Peter's words. In 1928, delegates representing Christian traditions from around the world met at Jerusalem for the first International Missionary Council convocation. They insisted that Christians should unite in common mission to the world. They also approved a statement that included these words about the centrality of Jesus Christ. "Jesus Christ, as the crucified and the living One, as Saviour and Lord, is also the center of the world-wide Gospel of the Apostles and the Church. Because He Himself is the Gospel, the Gospel is the message of the Church to the world. It is more than a philosophical theory; more than a theological system; more than a program for material betterment. The Gospel is rather the gift of a new world from God to this old world of sin and death; still more, it is the victory over sin and death, the revelation of eternal life in Him who has knit together the whole family in heaven and on earth in the communion of saints, united in the fellowship of service, of prayer, and of praise."[6]

The church's mission is to be faithful to that message in its witness, its life, and its action. We do not keep such good news to ourselves but must "Go therefore and make disciples of all nations, baptizing them in the name of the Father and of the Son and of the Holy Spirit, and teaching them to obey everything that I have commanded you" (Matt. 28:19-20 NRSV). As the church preaches the gospel, as it teaches and worships, as it celebrates baptism and the Lord's Supper, and as it practices what it preaches, it fulfills its missionary task. The missionary calling of the church is both a faithfulness to gospel teachings and a commitment to gospel life.

This idea of commitment means that everyone who claims Christ is on mission in the world. All Christians are on a missionary journey, wherever they live and whatever their vocation. We know and say that all believers are on mission, but we act as if missions is a special compartment of Christian ministry and action. Certainly some have a unique calling for specific missionary action, but that must not obscure the calling we all share.

Earlier generations of Christians sought ways to affirm the calling of all believers to participate in some facet of the church's mission wherever they might be. Seventeenth-century Quakers affirmed that all Christians were called to ministry through the "inner light" of Christ that dwelt within every individual. Christ's light was no respecter of persons, and God did "pour out [His] spirit on all flesh" at Pentecost (Acts 2:16-17 NRSV). All were compelled and empowered to declare the gospel wherever they might be.

Some early seventeenth-century Baptists utilized the laying on of hands as a powerful symbol of the missionary journey for every Christian. They used the laying on of hands in two ways. First, they administered it to all the new believers at baptism as a sign of the Holy Spirit's presence and as a reminder that all Christians were "ordained" to witness and minister. They also laid hands on those whom they set aside for specific missions in the community of faith.

Martin Luther, the great Protestant reformer, also emphasized the common calling and mission of all Christians. Luther refused to distinguish between callings for Christians. Whatever their specific vocations, all Christians were called to live according to the gospel and declare it by their daily lives. In his biography of Luther, Roland Bainton wrote that, "Luther never tired of defending those callings which for one reason or another were disparaged. The mother was considered lower than the virgin. Luther replied that the mother exhibits the pattern of the love of God, which overcomes sins just as her love overcomes dirty diapers."[7] Luther himself wrote, "The soldier boasts that it is hard work to ride in armor and endure heat, frost, dust, and thirst. But I'd like to see a horseman who could sit the whole day and look into a book. . . . As for schoolteaching, it is so strenuous that no one ought to be bound to it for more than ten years."[8]

All God's people are on mission together. In this book, we will explore the nature of the Christian mission as it relates to challenge, identity, and more specifically, risk. We celebrate the riskiness of the Christian faith for all who claim it.

The examples used in this book are those of persons who faced the challenge of life in various time periods and contexts. Throughout the book, every effort has been made to allow the representatives of the Christian mission to speak for themselves. This book contains what historians call primary source documents. It includes passages taken directly from the subjects in question and their original documents. The book attempts to explain the diversity of the missionary calling, as well as the varied responses individuals have made to specific situations of missions. Through their own written reflections we discover the many ways in which these servants of God sought to communicate their thoughts and feelings about the gospel and its accompanying risks and realities.

Let us not forget that some of the people cited here were sent out for specific ministries at home and abroad. Others fulfilled their calling through a variety of vocations. They, like those earliest Christians, could confess with Paul: "As God's servants, we try to recommend ourselves in all circumstances by our steadfast endurance: in distress, hardships, and dire straits; flogged, imprisoned, mobbed; overworked, sleepless, starving. We recommend ourselves by the innocence of our behaviour, our grasp of truth, our patience and kindliness; by gifts of the Holy Spirit, by sincere love, by declaring the truth, by the power of God. We wield the weapons of righteousness in right hand and left. Honour and dishonour, praise and blame, are alike our lot: we are the impostors who speak the truth, the unknown men whom all men know; dying we still live on; disciplined by suffering, we are not done to death; in our sorrows we have always cause for joy; poor ourselves we bring wealth to many; penniless, we own the world" (2 Cor. 6:4-10 NEB).

Is that *our* heritage, too?

For Discussion

1. In light of this chapter, write your own definition of Christian missions.
2. What common elements are evident in the three quotations that introduce this chapter?
3. The quotations from William Owen Carver and John R. Mott were written over 60 years ago. Are they applicable for the twenty-first century? Why?
4. What are ways Christians can respond to God's call in Matthew 28:19-20?

The Risk 2 of Faith

In the early days of the race to the moon, the astronauts took tremendous risks. They were going places where no one had gone; they were doing things no one had done. It was an exciting time, but great risk was involved in everything they did. Had all the people who worked on the equipment made the right calculations? Had all of the information been processed correctly? We learned from the Challenger accident that the risk was quite real. We learned that all the precautions they took were not enough. We learned that plowing new ground is always a risk.

Jesus recognized that, didn't He? Jesus used the idea of risk as a significant element of the stories He told and the points He made about the nature of the gospel life. Nowhere is this more evident than in His parables. In Matthew's Gospel we are confronted by a parable that Jesus told involving big money, financial speculation, and judgment. Through it all, there is the question of risk. He used those details to describe citizenship in God's kingdom.

Have you ever noticed how many of Jesus' parables involve economics? A son cashes in his inheritance and squanders it in a flash; a woman tears the house apart looking for a lost coin. A nameless man is robbed and left for dead and a Samaritan (of all people) saves him, carries him to safety, and leaves money to pay the medical bills. Then there is the story (Matt 25:14-30) about financial speculation—risk—on a grand scale.

You remember the story. A business man called in three of his employees, gave each a sum of money, and instructed them to do something with it while he was away. Two servants invested the money with great success while the third hid it for fear he would do the wrong thing. When the employer returned there was a day of reckoning. Two were rewarded, while the other was judged harshly. What a story!

Did Jesus realize that using the word "cash" was a sure-fire way of getting folks' attention in the first or the twenty-first century? Of course He did. It works every time.

To begin, I must confess that I have never really cared much for this parable and have seldom used it in sermons or lectures. But the gospel forces us to think about the "hard sayings" of Jesus and the implications for our lives. Perhaps my aversion to this parable began as a child when I heard this story in Sunday School and remembered the cigar box in my closet where I hid the money I saved from selling soft drink bottles and dealing in comic books with my barber, Bert McClean, who had the best comic book collection of the three barbers in Decatur, Texas. I knew I was in trouble with God for hiding my "talents" in the closet, so I avoided this parable whenever possible. Dealing with the risk of faith, however, compelled me to confront this story and its insights head on, without a safety net.

Matthew sets the parable in the middle of two others that also relate to the nature of the kingdom and the reality of final judgment. This parable, like the one about wise and foolish virgins that precedes it, begins with the sentence that can be paraphrased something like this: "when the day of judgment comes, the kingdom of heaven will be like this." And judgment it is, for all the protagonists.

A wealthy gentleman called in three servants/employees and told them that he was going away, probably for a long time. He then gave each of them cash money—big bucks for which they were responsible. The money was given in three different amounts dependent on the ability of each servant, but even the smallest sum was huge by anybody's standards. A talent, as the *King James Version Bible* calls the cash in this financial deal, refers to economics, not abilities. A talent was a substantial sum roughly equivalent to $2,000, give or take a few bucks for inflation and recession. He asked those employees to take care of the money for him. Time passed, certain events transpired, and the executive/master returned and the day of reckoning arrived. "What have you done with my money?" he inquired.

"Well," say two of the employees, "we put it to work." "We invested it. We put it in mutual funds, Fannie Maes, municipal bonds, and a few CD's, just don't ask us about the condominium fiasco. And, thank goodness, boss, you stayed away so long, we were able to double your money."

"Well done, fellows," said the CEO. "Here are the keys to the executive washroom. You get even greater responsibility because of your faithfulness in this matter."

The third employee had a problem, however. He was scared, scared that the boss man was a ruthless rogue who would ruin him if he lost one penny of the money he had given him. The huge amount of money and the possibilities for failure were so great that the man would not risk anything for his master. Rather, he buried the cash in a coffee can in the back yard, staying up half the night, perhaps, worrying that the yard worker or the mail carrier might stumble on it.

When the boss man found out what his employee had done he lived up to his reputation as a hard taskmaster. "You lazy rascal," he said to the servant. "You are right in your assessment of me, and because you failed you will learn first-hand how terrible I can be." He took away the man's money and dismissed him. Indeed, the Scripture is quite graphic. "Fling the useless servant out into the dark, the place of wailing and grinding of teeth!" (Matt. 25:30*b* NEB). Gruesome ending, isn't it? Apparently risk is a major element in the life of the kingdom.

Jesus could tell a story, couldn't He? He gets us all

interested in the dirt in other peoples' lives and all of a sudden without really knowing how it happened, we realize that we're the ones He's talking about. What exactly is going on in this strange little parable, and what does it mean to a bunch of economic, if not spiritual, capitalists like ourselves? Obviously, Jesus used the language of economics to teach some lessons about God's kingdom. For me, the primary point is this: Faith is a risk, pure and simple. The gospel of Jesus Christ involves great risks. Faith is an intriguing combination of certainty and risk. Risk is at the heart of the Christian mission. With that in mind, let's hold this story up, shake it a bit, and see what falls out.

First, as with most of Jesus' parables, this story has a great deal to do with the nature of faith itself. The servants have two different interpretations of the gift, the grace, they receive. Two of them accept the gift as something entrusted to them. The important word here is *entrusted*. The grace entrusted to them is to be used, shared, acted on, and offered responsibly in the world.

Remember that the earliest hearers and readers of this story in the first Christian churches believed that God's kingdom was just around the corner, that the risen Christ would return at any moment. But Jesus tarried, and in the interim, what were they to do? They had been entrusted with the gospel, and it was to be multiplied. They were the new incarnation of Christ, ambassadors for Him in the world. In a sense, this is a parable about what to do until the kingdom comes. While we wait on the kingdom, the Spirit of Christ calls us to take a chance, to risk everything, for grace.

The other side of the story, however, involves the so-called "wicked" servant. Why did the boss man call him wicked? It was not because he tried to cheat the master, but rather because he was irresponsible in his use or nonuse of the master's gift. Instead of accepting the gift as a trust to be used and multiplied, this guy couldn't get beyond his fear of his master.

As the renowned New Testament scholar, Eduard Schweizer, says, the servant is less interested in serving his

master than in protecting "his own skin."[1] He did nothing with
the gift, but instead hid it in the ground for fear he would
make a mistake, lose the money, and face his boss's wrath.
He could not handle the trust his boss had placed in him, so
he ran from responsibility. He looked inward, not outward,
and kept the gift to himself, hiding it for safekeeping. His spiritual and economic impotence, his failure to take the risk, cost
him everything.

What about us? What does God's grace mean to us? Does
it free us to strike out in new ventures, new hope, new liberation? Does grace control us or do we try to control grace?
What kind of grace do we hold in our hands? Do we understand that grace is an entrusting of goodness, gentleness,
patience—all the fruits of the Spirit—or is it something that
immobilizes us with fear?

Second, the kind of grace evident in this parable is a risk
pure and simple. The faithful servants in this story play the
odds, play the market, and put the money to use in ways that
will render a return, but always with the possibility that they
may lose their shirts, their jobs, even themselves. The wicked
servant on the other hand, refused to take the risk. Schweizer
comments, "[H]e is a man who cannot venture his own person, who cannot risk his own prosperity for the sake of his
lord's."[2] Because he would not risk for the kingdom, he was
wicked.

Many of Jesus' parables have a great deal to do with the
risk of faith. In the parable of the prodigal son, the boy risked
everything in hopes that his father would take him back. The
father risked the possibility of his son hitting the road again
as soon as he got his fill of steak and lobster tail, or bought
new batteries for his portable radio. But they both risked failure and rejection for the sake of love and grace. The
Samaritan took a chance that if he helped the injured man, he
too would be mugged. The two faithful servants in the text
took the chance that they might lose all that money, put it into
a first-century savings and loan somewhere, and have nothing to show for their trouble. What then? But they chose to
take the risk that the master would return and they would be

faithful to the responsibility, the gift, he had given them. In a sense, by faith, we are ever risking everything on grace. We reach out for it, grabbing it as we go down the third time, almost swamped with the pain and struggle, the hurt and hunger of life, hoping against hope that it will hold us up and get us through. We risk, with only moments to spare, that God really is there, that God really does care, and that grace will carry us through the journey. But we cannot merely be told that grace will work; we cannot intellectualize our way to grace. We cannot receive grace on the basis of somebody else's promises. We must experience it for ourselves; each of us must take that leap of faith toward God. For some that leap is a few wobbly baby steps, uncertain yet determined. For others, risking everything on grace means flinging ourselves over the Grand Canyon of life's broken promises, cheated moments, and false starts.

We don't simply risk everything *on* grace, we risk everything *with* it, as well. Grace is the inheritance we carry with us as Christ's people in the world. It is the commodity of the gospel. The essence of the gospel is not about getting a dose of grace and spending our lives guarding it. It is about receiving a gift that we then proceed to risk in response to the needs around us. Grace leads us to risk ourselves in the mission of the gospel. Grace flings us out into the world where only God knows what will happen to us. And there's always a bit of a risk to it: that the grace we offer in Christ's name will be misinterpreted, misunderstood, troublesome, even controversial, at times. Fearing all that, we are tempted to keep it properly protected, perhaps even hidden. By hiding grace, holding on to it, burying it, we hope to keep away from the hurt, the misunderstanding, and the controversy. But in trying to keep bad things from happening, nothing happens. Grace cautiously protected is grace wasted. That is one of the lessons of this parable.

Third, risking everything with or on grace means learning to deal with fear. The servant in the story was paralyzed by fear. He was afraid he'd lose the treasure, anger his master, and break the rules. So he horded the gift and that became his undoing. He wanted, as Schweizer says, an "absolute security"[3] which none of us can possess. Grace must give us the courage to risk, to dare, to take a chance for the gospel's sake. If we try to protect the gospel, fence it in, cover it up, build a wall around it, or toss it down some hole, we will destroy it in the process and let it slip from our fingers.

Do we really see the difference in the characters in this story? Two of them risked losing everything and wound up getting it all; one held on so tightly that he lost what he had tried to protect. Only when we turn grace loose, try it out, give it away, yes, when we risk losing it do we discover its secret. Schweizer writes that a religion "concerned only with not doing anything wrong in order that its practitioners may one day stand vindicated ignores the will of God."[4] The gift of God's love and grace, he says, is "never passively possessed."[5] To take a chance with grace and faith is to know that we may fail, make the wrong choice, embark on a mission which may not work after all. It is the risk the early disciples took when they met and followed Jesus of Nazareth along the shores of Galilee. It is a risk, isn't it? Living like that is a frightening chance to take.

The people who shape the church's mission are the people who choose to risk. Consider the early church and the Apostle Paul. Imagine the risk the early Christians took in learning to trust the leadership of a person who once tried to destroy them. Consider how much risk it took to accept him, believe in him, and listen to his message. Accepting Paul into the Christian church, and as an apostle at that, was risky business.

Also try to imagine the risk involved in Paul's idea that Gentiles could receive the gospel without becoming Jewish in the process. Consider the radical nature of a faith that even included Gentiles! Surely there were sincere Christians of Jewish heritage who were convinced that Paul's efforts would destroy, not promote, the faith. Yet Paul would write to the Galatians: "We ourselves are Jews by birth and not Gentile sinners; yet we know that a person is justified not by the works of the law but through faith in Jesus Christ" (Gal. 2:15-

16 NRSV). Paul laid his life on the line that Gentiles might
receive the good news of Jesus Christ. The Gentile church
began as a radical risk, and we are all the better for it. That
radical act, now taken for granted by the church, reminds us
again of the riskiness of the gospel on the way to the kingdom of God. Perhaps the gift of the gospel lies in giving us
the security, the strength, and the courage to risk new ministries, new commitments to witness, and new ways of reaching out to hurting persons.

Jesus said it, "For those who want to save their lives will
lose it, and those who lose their life for my sake will find it"
(Matt 16:25 NRSV). That sounds like a serious risk, doesn't it?

Risking everything on grace takes many forms and confronts us in many situations. Risk is an inescapable element
of the missionary calling. To follow Christ on mission in the
world (as all Christians are called to do) is to confront the
great risks of life and faith. Such risk is evident throughout the
history of Christ's church.

We find it in the calling of persons to respond to the missionary task. William Carey, the "father of modern missions,"
as he is sometimes known, chose to challenge one powerful
segment of Baptist theological opinion in his call to take the
gospel to all the world. Many were hesitant, charging that
such a missionary endeavor was a form of works/righteous-
ness in which human beings took on themselves the work of
God. However, Carey pressed on. In his famous sermon, "An
Enquiry into the Obligations of Christians to Use Means for
the Conversion of the Heathens," published in England in
1792, Carey called Baptists to accept the risk of fulfilling
Christ's Great Commission. He wrote: "Our Lord Jesus Christ,
a little before his departure, commissioned his apostles to
'Go, and teach all nations' "; or, as another evangelist
expresses it, " 'Go into all the world, and preach the gospel
to every creature.' " This commission was as extensive as
possible, and laid them under obligation to disperse themselves into every country of the habitable globe, and preach
to all the inhabitants, without exception or limitation."[6] In
spite of opposition, Carey pressed on, leading the way him-

self as a missionary to India. Others followed. We are heirs of his risky vision.

Others, less well known to us, also persevered in the face of discouragement from fellow Christians. Zilpha Elaw was an African-American woman born to free parents near Philadelphia. Sometime around 1790, she found her freedom and heard God's call to witness and ministry. Converted in a camp meeting in 1817, she began a ministry as a traveling preacher-evangelist. In 1840 she paid her own way on shipboard to England, convinced of God's call to declare God's Word in that land as a missionary-preacher. In her little-known and often overlooked memoirs, Elaw tells of her journey to England and her willingness to risk herself in the face of ridicule and controversy, all for a mission which God had instructed her to undertake. She wrote: "Soon after my arrival, I met with a gentleman, who advised my immediate return to my own country; adding that if he had been in America before my departure and had known of my intention, he would have advised me better: I replied, that I had no will of my own in the matter; but my heavenly Father commanded, and I durst not confer with flesh and blood, but obeyed and came: but like other men destitute of faith in God, he did not comprehend this kind of argument; and persisted in his worldly reasonings, saying that people did not give away their gold here, and I had much better return. It is to be deplored that there are so many Christians of this person's cast: who are of the world; speak in accordance with its principles and sentiments, and walk according to its course. . . . Having parted with this Laodicean gentleman, I called upon Mrs. H., in Princes-square: and my mind being somewhat damped, I sat a few minutes in silence, which Mrs. H. broke by an affectionate inquiry into my circumstances; at the same time, presenting me with a handsome donation; telling me not to be discouraged, for the Lord would open my way and sustain me: my mind was cheered and my faith strengthened by this opportune proofe [sic] of the power of God to furnish succours and raise up friends for his people even in a land of strangers."[7]

I include this rather lengthy excerpt from Zilpha Elaw's memoirs for several reasons. First, because it illustrates the sense of mission that this female missionary-preacher demonstrated over 150 years ago. Second, because her words reflect the sense of destiny and risk that she and other missionaries experienced. They believed that they had received a mandate from God to declare the gospel. They were willing to *risk* their lives in response to such a call, even when others rejected them. Third, because Zilpha Elaw's story—little known by most students of American missions—illustrates the fact that beyond the well-known heroes of Christian missions there were innumerable individuals who offered their lives to God for the sake of sharing the gospel. They went out to other lands, cultures, and peoples, often at their own expense, because they could not repudiate the word of God burning in their hearts and lives. Had you ever heard of Zilpha Elaw before? Well, now you have. She accepted the risk of faith and went out. In fact, we do not know what happened to her after her trip to England. Perhaps she returned to America, perhaps not. God knows. The call continues.

We hear that call in the words of martyrs and missionaries from the beginning of the church. Paul wrote that he was willing to risk everything for the sake of knowing Christ. As he said it: "I count everything sheer loss, because all is far outweighed by the gain of knowing Christ Jesus my Lord, for whose sake I did in fact lose everything" (Phil 3:8 NEB).

Polycarp, the second century Christian martyr, risked everything, even life itself, on faith in Christ. An aged man, Polycarp faced execution for his refusal to worship at the shrine of the Roman emperor (thus charged by Rome with atheism). An ancient document recounts the details of his death in A.D. 156. "The [Roman] Proconsul continued insisting and saying, 'Swear [an oath to Caesar], and I will release you; curse Christ.' And Polycarp said, 'Eighty-six years have I served Him, and He has done me no wrong: how then can I blaspheme my King who saved me?' "[8]

Polycarp's story reflects the beginnings of the church and its missionary imperative. The 2,000 years of Christian history detail the risk of the gospel as accepted and obeyed by innumerable saints and servants who cast everything on Christ and set out on mission in the world, some paying with their lives due to illness, fatigue, and even martyrdom. Polycarp was only one of the first of the martyrs. Others would follow, even into the twentieth century. In fact, missiologist David Barrett says that some 40 million Christians have been martyred since the New Testament period. From the eighteenth through much of the twentieth century, in certain tropical regions of the world, the life expectancy of western missionaries was little more than two years. In their book, *Missionaries,* Julian Pettifer and Richard Bradley write of those difficult conditions: "The cemeteries are full of memorials showing that many [missionaries] did not outlast the year of their arrival."[9]

One such cemetery illustrates the truth of that statement. The Protestant cemetery on the island of Macao contains innumerable memorials to missionaries who went out to Asia. Some, as the memorials note, were lost at sea through storms and shipwrecks. Others were killed by pirates, while others died of disease. Today the cemetery is located outside the walls of the old city since foreign Protestants were not allowed to be buried inside the city. Some missionaries had to be buried under cover of darkness for fear of the authorities. Missionary martyrdoms are not left in the distant past. We need only recall the memory of missionary women killed in Central America or Protestant missionaries held hostage in the Middle East to know that the risk of danger and death are continuing realities.

The possibility of martyrdom was not lost on many of the early missionaries. They seem to have recognized the costliness of their calling. Again, Pettifer and Bradley observe of those missionaries who first went out from Europe and America: "These were men driven by a burning, blind commitment. Count Zinzendorf, the greatest of eighteenth-century missionaries, said, 'I have one passion. It is He and He alone.' Melville Cox, who died after just four months in Liberia, is supposed to have uttered these last words, 'Let a thousand fall before Africa be given up.' On arriving in India, Henry Martyn said, 'Now let me burn out for God.' Of Hudson Taylor, founder of the China Inland Mission, it was said that never once in fifty years did the sun rise in China without finding him on his knees."[10] Theirs was a powerful recognition of the riskiness of the calling to take the gospel to the world.

Since it is a risk, this wonderful gospel, then let us get a little audacious in our living of it—let us not fear to take a chance, to cultivate a bit of gospel eccentricity from time to time. Surely the gospel gives us courage to take a risk on some new ministries, new paradigms, new and surprising responses to the unbearable needs about us.

Jesus said it, didn't He? "For those who want to save their life will lose it, and those who lose their life for my sake, and for the gospel, will save it" (Mark 8:35 NRSV). Sounds like a risk to me. What do you think?

For Discussion

1. How does the idea of risk influence your understanding of the Christian journey?
2. What, in your opinion, is an appropriate definition of grace? of faith?
3. What is the relationship between faith, grace, and risk?
4. How does the parable discussed in this story (Matt. 25) influence or affect your own life?
5. Is Eduard Schweizer correct when he suggests that none of us can possess "absolute security"?
6. Compare the quotes from William Carey and Zilpha Elaw. What do they tell you about the call to missions?

The Risk of 3 Identity

"Why do you make so much fuss over baptism?" the college student asked. He was sitting in a religion class on the first day of the new semester. "Faith is the important thing," he continued, "and if you have faith, that's all that matters. After all, baptism is only a symbol."

"So when it comes to baptism you can take it or leave it?" I inquired.

"Sure," he replied.

"And by any chance, are you a Baptist?" I asked, anticipating his answer.

"Sure," he said.

As a university religion professor, I experience that response or similar ones from Christian students with alarming frequency. Many are not certain as to the central elements of the Christian faith and the meaning of past traditions and heritage. Whether they realize it or not, they are confronting the issue of Christian identity.

On one hand, the young man in my class was correct. Faith is the heart of Christian identity. There is no Christian life apart from faith in Jesus Christ. But to make Christian baptism a negotiable, as if we could take it or leave it, especially for folks who claim the name Baptist, is to diminish Christian

identity considerably. To say that baptism is a symbol is to confess that it has great power for the church and the individual.
Thus baptism is not merely a symbol; rather, it is an event that
shapes our common identity in Christ. Remember Paul's words
to the church at Corinth? "For Christ is like a single body with
its many limbs and organs, which, many as they are, together
make up one body. For indeed we were all brought into one
body by baptism, in the one Spirit, whether Jews or Greeks,
whether slaves or free men, and that one Holy Spirit was
poured out for all of us to drink" (1 Cor. 12:12-13 NEB).

Symbols have great power in our lives. Symbols are
sources of identity. They help us know who we are and where
we fit. The early Christians recognized that reality when they
celebrated baptism, shared in the Lord's Supper, and carried
out the laying on of hands, along with other outward and visible signs of the inward and spiritual grace of God. Today's
Christians face a major threat, not simply from secularism,
materialism, and other modern temptations, but from the loss
of identity among the people of God. In a real sense, there is
no generic Christianity. At its best, Christianity demands that
we be quite specific regarding faith and baptism, salvation and
community, ministry and witness. Identity provides people
with a foundation, a place to stand, from which to reach out
to a needy world. Identity links the individual to a specific
community of persons who have chosen to live out the gospel
in specific ways, to express the gospel mandates in particular
rites, beliefs, and actions.

To many contemporary Christians, many of the Church's
observances seem incidental if not downright obsolete.
Sunday to Sunday, year to year, sermons are preached, baptism and the Lord's Supper are administered, and missionaries
are sent out, all in a rather commonplace, even predictable
fashion. In fact, such activities may become so commonplace
that observers and participants alike may forget the risk
behind the most basic elements of Christian identity. This is
particularly true in times of religious transition and reorgani-
zation. We are currently experiencing such a time.

As the twenty-first century begins, American churches are

reexamining and redefining the nature of religious organizations. For over two centuries, denominations have served as
the primary form of religious organization in American life.
Today, however, fewer and fewer religious Americans think of
their primary religious identity in terms of a denominational
identity. That may mean that religious Americans are more
open to Christian brothers and sisters in various groups and
that old competitions and hatreds are moderating. It may also
mean the loss of an understanding of the basic sources of
Christian belief and tradition.

Historian Martin E. Marty illustrates this dilemma when he
cites a statement from the pastor of a large evangelical congregation in Michigan. The pastor described the baptismal pol-
icy in his church as follows: "We immerse adults to baptize
them, but we also sprinkle adults if that's what they want. We
baptize infants, but we also dedicate infants if people want
that instead. We'll back-flip someone into the pool if that's
what they really want. . . . We don't want baptism to become
a barrier that would keep anyone from Christianity."[1]

While the pastor is sincere in his concern to move his
focus from the mode of baptism to the faith behind baptism,
he may also overlook the profound impact of baptism and
other Christian symbols as sources of identity. Indeed, baptism may even represent a "barrier" for those who choose to
turn from one way of life to another in order to accept Christ
and His mission in the world. We might even suggest that
Christian baptism is one of the most basic methods for determining Christian identity. In the early days of the church,
baptism was the outward and visible sign that divided
Christian from pagan. To choose it was often to break with
the past and begin anew. Baptism has been a risky action
from the beginning.

The Apostle Paul frequently reminded his readers of the
importance, the riskiness, of Christian baptism. As he
described it, baptism was more than simply a washing with
water. It was a sign that persons had literally put on Christ like
a garment. He wrote, "For as many of you as have been baptized into Christ have put on Christ" (Gal. 3:27 KJV). Putting

on Christ also brought a new identity that broke down old divisions. As Paul said, "There is neither Jew nor Greek, there is neither slave nor free, there is neither male nor female; for you are all one in Christ Jesus" (Gal. 3:28 RSV).

For the early Christians, baptism was certainly a barrier that often cut them off from family, friends, and citizenship. To receive baptism, to identify with the community of Christian faith, was to leave behind the old and turn to the new. It could mean the loss of possessions, as well as persecution, imprisonment, and even death—risky business all around.

Likewise, participation in that other profound source of Christian identity, the Lord's Supper, was at times risky for the earliest followers of Jesus. Just outside the city of Rome are the catacombs, those ancient burial places where Christians often gathered for worship. In those underground caves the Roman Christians celebrated the Lord's Supper in secret, lest they be arrested by the Roman government. Sometimes the bread and wine were laid out on the tops of tombs. In other words, the tombs became the table! There, surrounded by the reminders of death, Christians remembered Christ's own death and resurrection, claiming that promise for themselves. There, they identified with His suffering and His call to "take up the cross," knowing that they, too, faced the possibility of arrest, imprisonment, and death. To receive the Lord's Supper was to remember who they were—the people of God, bound together by faith in Christ. Through the Lord's Supper, they were united to Christ and to each other. Hidden in the catacombs, Christians affirmed the blessing and the risk of their identity.

The people of God have often risked everything for the sake of identity. Identity is an essential part of the church's mission. Those who declare the gospel are inviting persons to accept a distinct and life-transforming character. This is certainly evident in the lives of those who accept a vocation as missionaries or ministers in the church. Sometimes the risk of identity confronts the missionaries themselves. They are forced to declare who they are and what Christianity means to them in specific ways.

Perhaps this is no more evident than in the story of Adoniram and Ann Hasseltine Judson and their decision to risk their very missionary calling by becoming Baptists. The Judsons and their colleague, Luther Rice, were sent out as missionaries to India by the American Board of Commissioners for Foreign Missions, an agency of Congregational churches in America. Departing in 1812, the three missionaries came to accept Baptist views aboard ship and were convinced that they could not in good conscience represent the Congregational Board. While Baptists and Congregationalists shared common doctrines on conversion, church government, witness, and ministry, they disagreed over the meaning and form of that powerful source of Christian identity, baptism. Likewise, in 1812 Baptists were still something of a scandalous sect compared to the staid, established, and respectable Congregationalists. Yet Rice and the Judsons were convinced of the importance of their newfound beliefs and were willing to risk their mission for these ideals.

Consider their plight. They arrived in a new land to establish a new mission having rejected their only visible means of support, the American Board of Commissioners for Foreign Missions, the Congregational mission society founded in 1810. The Baptists to whose beliefs they had "converted" had no similar mission society to offer them necessary funds. Indeed, many Baptists were uncertain as to whether the sending of missionaries was at all appropriate. Some believed that mission boards were unscriptural while others felt that missionary activity violated God's sovereignty to save persons without human intervention.

The new Baptist missionaries were forced to send Luther Rice back to the United States to implore Baptists to support their endeavor. It was a serious risk to take so far away from the United States. Rice was successful but not without great debate. The Triennial Convention, the first national missionary society founded by Baptists, was begun in 1814.

Ann Hasseltine Judson's correspondence reveals that she and her husband knew exactly the risk they were taking for the sake of a new Christian identity. In one wonderful letter to a friend, she describes their decision and its implications. Dated September 7, 1812, it began: "Can you, my dear Nancy, still love me, still desire to hear from me, when I tell you I have become a Baptist? If I judge from my own feelings, I answer, you will, and that my differing from you in those things which do not affect our salvation will not diminish your affection for me, or make you unconcerned for my welfare."[2]

She noted that the decision evolved "prayerfully" over a period of months, and that "an examination of the subject of baptism" began on board the Caravan, the ship that carried her and her husband to India. Adoniram Judson, reading the Greek New Testament, began to question infant baptism as practiced among the Congregationalists and other evangelical denominations.

Ann Judson responded to her husband's doubts, sometimes playing devil's advocate. She wrote to her friend Nancy that she herself was hesitant. "I felt afraid he would become a Baptist, and frequently urged the unhappy consequences if he should." She even reported that she took the "Pedobaptist side" (infant baptism), even as she began to have her own doubts. Eventually both Judsons accepted Baptist doctrines. Of that decision, Ann Judson wrote to her friend: "Thus, my dear Nancy, we are confirmed Baptists, not because we wished to be, but because truth compelled us to be. We have endeavored to count the cost, and be prepared for the many severe trials resulting from this change of sentiment. We anticipate the loss of reputation, and of the affection and esteem of many of our American friends. . . . These things, my dear Nancy, have caused us to weep and pour out our hearts to Him whose directions we so much wish and need. We feel that we are alone in the world, with no real friend but each other, no one on whom we can depend but God."[3]

Adoniram Judson also described his change of heart regarding the nature of baptism and its impact on his life and his mission. For him, as for his wife, it was not an easy decision. In 1812 he wrote to Lucius Bolles, pastor of First Baptist Church, Salem, Massachusetts, explaining his decision and asking for Baptist support. "Within a few months, I have experienced an entire change of sentiments on the subject of baptism. My doubts concerning the correctness of my former system of belief, commenced during my passage from America to this country; and after many painful trials, which none can know but those who are taught to relinquish a system in which they had been educated, I settled down in the full persuasion that the immersion of a professing believer in Christ is the only Christian baptism. Mrs. Judson is united with me in this persuasion. We have signified our views and wishes to the Baptist missionaries at Serampore, and expect to be baptized in this city next Lord's day."[4]

This amazing correspondence from the hand of both the Judsons is filled with the language of risk—risk inseparably linked to a specific choice of specific expression of Christianity. The Judsons realized that Christianity itself is not simply a generic religion. It has identity, varied identity to be sure, but identity, nonetheless. Their lives illustrate the powerful impact of identity within the Christian community. Yet it was not an identity that turned them against their former Congregational colleagues. Again, Ann Judson wrote that "the most trying circumstance attending this change, and that which has caused us the most pain, is the separation which must take place between us and our dear [former] missionary associates."[5]

In the case of the Judsons, their convictions regarding Baptist identity did not lead them to arrogance or a feeling of superiority in response to their former colleagues. They did not condemn their Congregational brothers and sisters. Rather, they were committed to their own convictions, remaining open to others who could not follow them into the Baptist family. Thus the identity of Christian community that we choose should not lead us to condemn others, but to reach out to them in Christian fellowship from the foundation of our own convictions and beliefs.

Baptists cultivated identity as they expanded their mission and ministry in America. As Baptists spread throughout the American frontier, they also established churches on the basis of an identity bound in baptismal immersion, the Lord's Supper, and the preaching of the Word. Reverend Z. N. Morrell described the first recorded services of baptism, the Lord's Supper, and preaching held by Baptists in Texas. Note the power of identity in his description. "Sunday morning at ten o'clock we met at the water, and after a short discourse on the subjects and action of baptism, nine converts testified their belief in the burial and resurrection of Jesus, by allowing themselves to be buried in and raised out of the water of the Colorado River. On retiring to a small house, with an arbor of brush built in front of it for the occasion, Brother Baylor, in his usual happy manner, preached a most excellent sermon. . . . This season of refreshing from the presence of the Lord greatly revived the drooping spirit of the way-worn traveler, and as we surrounded the table, with Brother Baylor and those dear brethren and ate the bread and drank the wine, my poor soul blessed God in faith that the waters of the Colorado would blossom as the rose, and that the solitary places along this fertile valley would one day be made glad."[6] In a new and unpredictable environment, some Christian believers reaffirmed their ancient identity and took strength from it.

Whatever else it may be or become, one important characteristic of the denomination has been its concern to communicate identity to a particular Christian community. In the period following the Revolutionary War, Americans needed a way to organize religious life in a new nation in which religious liberty was the norm and where state churches no longer existed. (Remember that New England, Virginia, and other segments of the original thirteen colonies had government-established churches.) When the old ways of ordering church life were less workable, Americans turned to a relatively new form of religious organization, the denomination. Denominations became the shape of Protestant life in America. They helped pass on identity to generations of Christian believers.

Peter Cartwright, the nineteenth-century Methodist circuit rider, described the Methodism he observed in frontier America in the year 1804. Consider the identity it communicated. "We had no pewed churches, no choirs, no organs; in a word, we had no instrumental music in our churches anywhere. The Methodists in that early day dressed plain;

attended their meetings faithfully, especially preaching, prayer and class meetings; they wore no jewelry, no ruffles; they would frequently walk three or four miles to class-meetings and home again, on Sundays. . . . They could, nearly every soul of them, sing our hymns and spiritual songs. They religiously kept the Sabbath day: many of them abstained from dram drinking, not because the temperance reformation was ever heard of in that day, but because it was interdicted in the General Rules of our Discipline. The Methodists of that day stood up and faced their preacher when they sung; they kneeled down in the public congregation as well as elsewhere, when the preacher said, 'Let us pray.' "[7]

By the end of his ministry, Cartwright was concerned that Methodists were losing their identity and distinctiveness. In the 1850s, he wrote: "Verily we have fallen on evil times. Is it possible that now, when we abound in education, that we need Biblical instruction more than when we had no education, or very little? . . . I awfully fear for our beloved Methodism."[8]

If Cartwright's concerns reveal anything, it is that the risk of identity is elusive. The church is compelled to find ways to pass on Christian identity from one generation to another. Such a legacy is not communicated casually, but requires that Christians and churches be intentional about what they believe, and how the most basic sources of Christianity are taught and promoted by the community of faith. Thus contemporary Christians, whatever their specific faith tradition, must affirm those sources of identity that provide a foundation for faith in both the present and the future. Such a challenge has never been easy.

Baptists and other American denominations have not always seen identity as something that can be shared and celebrated by various Christian groups. Nineteenth-century Protestants often competed with each other, believing that the risk of identity set them against each other. Many groups—Baptists, Methodists, Presbyterians, Disciples of Christ, and others—claimed to be the only true churches of Christ, to the exclusion of other communions.

Again, Peter Cartwright, the outspoken representative of frontier Methodist missions, was an articulate spokesman for

Methodist theology. He was at once the great preacher and competitor in the struggle to set forth specific identity among religious groups in the frontier wilderness. In 1813 he wrote: "We (Methodists) preached in new settlements, and the Lord poured out his Spirit, and we had many convictions and many conversions. It was the order of the day, (though I am sorry to say it,) that we were constantly followed by a certain set of proselyting Baptist preachers. These new and wicked settlements were seldom visited by these Baptist preachers until the Methodist preachers entered them; then, when a revival was gotten up, or the work of God revived, these Baptist preachers came rushing in, and they generally sung their sermons . . . in substance it was 'water!' 'water!' 'You must follow your blessed Lord down into the water.' Indeed, they made so much ado about baptism by immersion, that the uninformed would suppose that heaven was an island, and there was no way to get there but by diving or swimming."[9]

This kind of competition was a way of drawing lines between Christians, each claiming to be more enlightened than the other group. We find it entertaining now, but then it was deadly serious. One group felt compelled to establish its own identity at the expense of another. The question facing contemporary Christians seems to be, Can we discover specific Christian identities without attacking each other? It is a formidable challenge.

The risk of identity involves the continued quest for balance in two powerful elements of Christian faith. On one hand, we must continually assert the importance of those specific beliefs and practices that inform, communicate, and engender Christian identity. We struggle with the meaning of faith and baptism, the nature of salvation and mission, and the shape that Christianity must take in our own lives. These convictions grow out of our understanding of the teaching of Scripture, our participation in the community of faith, the church, and our own experience of the gracious presence of God. We are called to discover a place to stand that identifies us with Christians past, present, and future. We can choose a heritage that offers us a source of stability and community. Yet, choosing a particular identity means selecting certain views over others—risky business, especially in matters of faith.

At the same time, such a conviction of specific Christian identity should not lead to pride and arrogance regarding our ideas. It should not cause us to turn inward on ourselves, cutting us off from others within the broader church of Christ, those whose views may be different from our own. Identity provides us with a place to stand from which to reach out in ministry and witness to others. Without specific Christian identity we are easy prey for those who might lead us who knows where. We are "tossed to and fro" by every changing wind and doctrine as Paul wrote in Ephesians 4:14 (KJV). When identity blinds us to others, we ignore the scriptural admonition that there is only "one Lord, one faith, one baptism, One God and Father of us all" (Eph. 4:5 KJV).

Some of the earliest "ecumenical encounters" (cooperation among various Christian groups) began on the mission field. William Carey, the father of the modern missions movement, was an early advocate of interdenominational cooperation and fellowship. While unashamedly Baptist in his own Christian, Baptist, and missionary identity, Carey did not hesitate to reach out to other Christian brothers and sisters in the spirit of cooperation and goodwill.

In 1806 Carey made a dramatic proposal for a gathering of Christian groups involved in the missionary endeavor. Some called it the "most startling missionary proposal of all time."[10] Carey wrote of it in a letter to the English Baptist leader Richard Fuller. "Would it not be possible to have a general association of all denominations of Christians, from the four quarters of the world, held there once in about ten years? I earnestly recommend this plan, let the first meeting be in the year 1810, or 1812 at the furthest. I have no doubt but it would be attended with many important effects. We could understand one another better, and more entirely enter into one another's views by two hours' conversation than by two or three years epistolary [written] correspondence."[11]

The suggestion was made but not acted on for another century. In 1910 the first International Missionary Conference

was held in Edinburgh, Scotland. It brought together representatives of Christian groups from all over the world. They
acknowledged their differences but affirmed their common
identity in Christ.

Carey's example has not always prevailed, however. We
also know that conviction can all too easily turn to bigotry and
arrogance. Most religious groups, including Baptists, have
acted in ways that alienated, even undermined, persons, over
issues of identity and belief. Living with identity and openness
is itself risky business. Our beliefs should keep us open to others who minister in Christ's name, even when their views dif-
fer from our own. It requires continued balance in our
attitudes and our relationships.

One of the great challenges facing contemporary Christians
concerns the issue of identity. If denominational and institutional
resources for teaching and passing on the faith are increasingly
less uniform or intact, Christian individuals and churches must be
intentional in their attempts to develop specific aspects of
Christian identity and nurture it in new generations of believers.
The renewed mission of the church is to affirm a specific identity regarding faith and baptism, law and gospel, grace and missions. At its best, that identity should make us more *intentional*
about our own specific Christian heritage, and more *cooperative*
with those of other Christian traditions, than we have ever been
before. Can we respond to such a challenge?

FOR DISCUSSION

1. In what ways do baptism and the Lord's Supper portray
   your own Christian identity?
2. What does the Judsons' decision to become Baptists say to
   you about the importance of Christianity identity and its
   accompanying risk?
3. How can you work to nurture a missions "identity" in the
   next generation of Christian believers?
4. How can diverse Christian traditions retain identity and
   cooperate together in the missions endeavor of the church?
5. What aspects of Christianity portray your identity as a Christian?

The Risk of Place

The sun had not yet risen when they started out across the desert. "I hope we got everything," the woman remarked.

"We took what we could," the man replied.

"Which way are we headed?" Sarai asked quietly.

"That way," her husband answered, pointing toward the distant horizon, "at least for today."

Was Abram's departure from his homeland, the place of his birth, something like that? Where was he going and when would he get there? How did it feel to follow the edict of God, "Leave your own country, your kinsmen, and your father's house, and go to a country that I will show you" (Gen. 12:1 NEB)? Risky business, faith, at least the way Abram experienced it.

Life began for the man named Abram somewhere out in the Arabian desert, at a place called Ur of the Chaldeans, located in what we call the Middle East. Abram's kinfolk lived all around that place, and, like most desert tribes, they were a pretty tight-knit clan. It must have been a decent place, at least Abram seems not even to have considered leaving until he received word to get on down the road. As the Genesis text says, "And so Abram set out as the Lord had bidden him" (Gen. 12:4a NEB). He left home and place,

security and family, and if he argued with God about it, the
text gives no indication.

He just left. He gathered up his immediate family—spouse
Sarai, nephew Lot, Lot's family, and "all the property they had
collected, and all the dependents they had acquired in
Harran, and they started on their journey to Canaan" (Gen.
12:5 NEB). Off they went and never looked back, except perhaps for Lot's wife, who may have made a habit of looking
back. Without batting an eye, Abram packed his bags and left
the safety of home for the uncertainty (and risk) of somewhere else—all because God told him to do so.

Some people call that wanderlust, I suppose, an obsessive
curiosity to find out what's on the other side of the next hill.
Some see it as consistent with the nomadic existence of a
desert people. Still others (myself included) would say it was
an act of faith. At least that is how the New Testament writer
saw it. It says in Hebrews, "By faith Abraham obeyed the call
to go out to a land destined for himself and his heirs, and left
home without knowing where he was to go. By faith he settled as an alien in the land promised him, living in tents, as
did Isaac and Jacob, who were heirs to the same promise. For
he was looking forward to the city with firm foundations,
whose architect and builder is God" (Heb. 11:8-10 NEB). The
way the Bible tells it, this was no mere whim. Abram did not
do this impulsively; he acted in faith. He took the risk. He
hoped it was true, wished it was true, and went out on faith
as if it were true, but not without risk. Home was a sure thing;
leaving home, even by faith, was not.

Christ's mission is just like that. Whether you go or stay,
whether you believe in God at home or on the interstate highway, faith is a risk. Abram is not the only example, is he? Saul,
a.k.a. Paul, had everything he wanted—prestige, power, education, and security—yet in a moment on the road to
Damascus he dropped everything. He lost it all for the last
place on earth he thought he would wind up, the church of
Jesus Christ. In the end, Paul left what he thought he could
not live without, all, as he said, for the "excellency of the
knowledge of Christ Jesus my Lord" (Phil. 3:8 KJV).

Such things still happen, I believe. People still risk their lives, or at least important segments thereof, for such a vision of the living God. They relinquish the security of one place for the insecurity and wonder of something else. They leave home and family, friends and roots, for the journey who knows where.

Faith really is risky business. So is growth and maturity, birth and rebirth. Faith, you see, inevitably involves the question of place. It means knowing, or hoping you know, when to go or when to stay, when to watch and pray, and when to launch out in some new and sometimes dangerous act of faith. Such faith may take us to places and circumstances we never thought possible.

Abram, like all of us, was seeking a place. He sought a place to discover God, to face life, to raise a family, and to put down roots. He looked for a place to belong, as well as a place to believe. Abram encountered God's presence and in response to that encounter went looking for a new place. By faith he risked the possibility that in leaving one place he would never really find another.

But he did find such a place, a place called Canaan, and in that new place Abram found a new name. Abram, whose name meant "high father," became Abraham, "father of a multitude." He became father of a new people, and for thousands of years that multitude, those children of Abraham, have understood something of their own identity in terms of the land of Canaan, even when they did not live there themselves. Indeed, Hebrew history and identity has been shaped by the land and the struggle to maintain it from Abraham's time to our own day.

Abraham's search for a place is an important aspect of the journey and risk of faith for all of us. Place is not merely geographical; it is also spiritual and personal. All persons search for a place where they belong, where they feel at home, and where they experience God's presence. Some people simply find that place more readily than others.

Why is it some people find their place almost from the beginning and never turn aside from that original vision? Faith comes to them through family, church, or personal experience. They hear and know, believe and live, and the place of their faith holds as years go by.

But what happens when the place won't hold anymore? What happens when, like Abraham, you know it's time to move on, or go somewhere else in obedience to God's command? How do we find the strength to move from one geographical or spiritual place to another? When you lose your place, do you lose your faith? What do you do when you are called beyond the safety and security of childhood locale or even childhood faith, to an arena of life and mission you have never been before? The story of the church's mission is the story of persons who have moved out, and moved on, in response to the God's call.

The call to missions is inseparable from the call to place. Sometimes we stay put, sometimes we move on in response to the divine mandate. It is risky, but it is the heart of the missionary calling and enterprise.

As a historian, I am struck by the importance of place in the lives of men and women across the centuries. I am also impressed by the way in which persons who felt a special call to missions had to deal with the nature of place—staying home, going out, returning home. I am struck also by the way in which the idea of place shapes the identity of those who stay with old places and those who feel compelled to head for new ones. In fact, the question of place is a significant element of missions. And place is always risky.

Those who follow the call to missions must deal with the question of place, whether they stay at home or hit the road. When we think of missionaries, we usually think of those who go out from home, from one place to another, from a more secure environment to an unknown and sometimes dangerous one. As they go out, those persons have to learn to come to terms with place in ways they may never have dreamed of before.

Coming to terms with place was true in the American experience. When one reads the journals and diaries of those early settlers and missionaries to and in America, one is struck by the way in which they struggled with the nature of place and its impact on themselves and the gospel they proclaimed. The risk of place is evident throughout.

Early missionaries to America often sent back word to other British and European Christians that they were needed in the effort to evangelize Native American peoples and participate in a great missionary enterprise. Alexander Whitaker was known as the missionary to Virginia. In 1613, Whitaker wrote a famous missionary treatise entitled "Good Newes from Virginia," in which he urged English Christians to come over and help in the evangelization of native peoples. Citing the text, "Cast thy bread upon the waters: for after many daies [days] thou shalt finde it," Whitaker wrote, "Let me turne your eyes, my brethren of England, to behold the waters of Virginia: where you may behold a fit subject for the exercise of your Liberalitie, persons enough on whom you may cast away your Bread, and yet not without hope, after many daies [days] to finde it. Yea, I will not feare to affirme unto you, that those men whom God hath made able any way to be helpeful to this Plantation, and made knowne unto them the necessities of our wants, are bound in conscience by vertue of this precept, to lay their helping hands to it, either with their purse, persons, or prayers, so farre forth as God hath made them fit for it. For it is evident that our wise God hath bestowed no gift upon any man, for their private use, but for the good of other men, whom God shall offer to their Liberalitie."[1]

Whitaker was convinced that this new place, Virginia, had been opened for the sake of the gospel. Thus he commented, "Wherefore, since God hath opened the doore of Virginia, to our countrey of England, wee are to thinke that God hath, as it were, by word of mouth called us in, to bestow our severall Charity on them [Native Americans]. And that this may be the better appeare, we have many reasons to encourage us to bee Liberall minded and open-handed toward them."[2]

Place carried significant responsibility for Christians. Whitaker sought to awaken a call in those who were far

away. He was not alone in that endeavor. Those who came
to America as missionaries confronted the reality of place in
the distant regions of the new land. Place was a struggle from
the beginning.

John Martin Mack (1715–1784) and his wife, Jeannette Rau
(1722-1749), were Moravian missionaries to the Native
American Indians. Jeannette was a linguist, fluent in the
Mohican language, a common tongue for many of the
Algonquin tribes. In the years 1741-1742 they were the first
missionaries to visit certain tribes in western Pennsylvania.
They did so in the company of the renowned Lutheran pietist,
Count Nicholas von Zinzendorf whom they referred to as the
"Disciple." Both John and Jeannette shared in the missionary
calling and endeavor.

John Mack's journal details their travels and illustrates the
relationship of missions to the issue of place. He wrote that,
"our way lay through the forest, over rocks and frightful
mountains, and across streams swollen by the recent heavy
rains. This was a fatiguing and dangerous journey, and on
several occasions we imperiled our lives in fording creeks,
which ran with impetuous current." The little group preached
and talked with the Indians, most of whom were Mohicans.
Mack wrote, "My Jeannette acted as interpreter of what
passed during the [preaching] meeting."[3]

He continued, "From our first encampment . . . I once
road out with the Disciple and Anna [an Indian convert].
There was a creek in our way, in a swampy piece of ground.
Anna and myself led in crossing, and with difficulty succeeded in ascending the farther bank, which was steep and
muddy. But the Disciple was less fortunate, for in attempting
to land, his horse plunged, broke the girth, and his rider
rolled off backwards into the water, the saddle upon him. It
required much effort on my part to extricate him, and when
I at last succeeded, he kissed me and said, 'My poor brother!
I am an endless source of trouble!' Being without change [of
clothes], we were necessitated to dry our clothes at the fire
and then brush off the mud. Adventures of this kind befell us
more than once."[4]

For these early American missionaries, place could be dangerous, simply through confrontation with a rugged frontier environment. The environment they entered was the place of another people, the Native American Indians, who often perceived the presence of these outsiders as little more than an invasion. Conflicts between these peoples over the nature and possession of the American "place" not only created political problems, but also spiritual problems as well. When armed conflict between Indians and settlers resulted in deaths, specifically the deaths of missionary families, a serious theological issue arose. Had God really called them to this strange and savage place? The answers varied.

Thomas Baldwin (1748-1835) was a layman and frontiersman whose entire family (his wife and three children) were killed as a result of Anglo Saxon and Native American Indian conflicts in Kentucky. As a result, he retired to the Kentucky wilderness where he wrote about the dangers and sorrows of that place and the role of religion in it all. As he observed the loss of his family in one place, he looked for that "blessed place" where they would be united once again. He hoped for heaven and a reunion. Baldwin observed that, "Religion consoles the aching heart of the afflicted, and reconciles the unhappy to their misfortunes—the grieved parent who has [buried] his earthly comfort, his beloved partner and darling children, in the bosom of the valley, is comforted and cheered by the flattering persuasions of Religion—he is assured by it that if he lives faithful to Christ, he shall revisit his beloved friends in that blessed place where dwells every felicity, and an antidote for every care and painful sensation."[5]

Missionaries such as Narcissa Whitman (1808-47) noted in their journals of the uniqueness of their mission in another wilderness place: Oregon Territory. She described the climate and the general setting among the Native Americans with whom she and her husband sought to work as Presbyterian missionaries. She even celebrated the birth of a daughter—a new life in a hostile environment. Tragedy was not far behind, however. The daughter drowned two years after her birth and the Whitmans themselves were killed by Cayuse Indians in 1847.

Her journal illustrates the setting and the calling. Even her words betray a sense of the hostile nature of their abode: "Wieletpoo [Waiilatpu] Jan 2 1837. Universal fast day. Through the kind Providence of God we are permitted to celebrate this day in heathen lands. It has been one of peculiar interest to us, so widely separated from kindred souls, alone, in the thick darkness of heathenism."

"Sab[bath] Jan 29. Our meeting to day with the Indians was more interesting than usual. I find that as we succeed in their language in communicating the truth to them so as to obtain a knowledge of their views & feelings, my heart becomes more & more interested in them."

"March 30th. Again I can speak of the goodness & mercy of the Lord to us in an especial manner. On the evening of my birthday March 14th we received the gift of a little Daughter a treasure invaluable. During the winter my health was very good, so as to be able to do my work. About a week before her birth I was afflicted with an inflammatory rash which confined me mostly to my room. After repeated bleeding it abated very considerably. I was sick but about two hours. She was born half past eight, so early in the evening that we all had time to get considerable rest that night."[6] Even in what seemed a "wilderness," life went on.

For some persons involved in missions, the problems of a new and uncertain place are never reconciled. This reality is illustrated in the experience of the two Moon sisters, Edmonia and Lottie, in nineteenth-century China. Edmonia Moon preceded her sister Lottie as a Southern Baptist missionary to China by almost one year. Only 21 years of age, "Eddie," as her friends called her, experienced profound culture shock. She was never able to adjust to the surroundings of that Asian place. In those days, newcomers to the mission field were given minimal preparatory training and guidance. They were expected to jump into the missionary work and sink or swim. Edmonia Moon's difficulties increased, even after her sister Lottie arrived in China. She had chronic health problems and received little sympathy from the veteran missionaries. Lottie

Moon's contrasting energy and rapid adaptation to the Chinese setting magnified her sister's difficulties. Finally, in 1875, Edmonia Moon returned to the United States. China was not a place she could make her own. Some places are not for everyone.[7]

Current missionary procedures make every effort to provide for such realities before persons move into ministry in places far and near. But the experiences of those two women illustrate that places are specific and unique. Not every person can live and work, minister and witness in every environment. Place is a risk. Not everyone can find a home in the same place.

Edmonia Moon's experience was not unique. Many persons who went out as missionaries struggled with the departure from home and the search for home in a new place. Peggy Dow offers an articulate account of those feelings in her diary. Peggy Dow was the wife of Lorenzo Dow, a well-known and somewhat eccentric evangelist of the late eighteenth and early nineteenth centuries. Dow was something of an independent with loose ties to the Methodists. He traveled throughout England and America, preaching and organizing churches, often calling himself the "eccentric cosmopolite," or traveler.

Peggy Dow's journal is one of the few written accounts of a woman married to an itinerant preacher in early nineteenth-century America and England. It is a fascinating account of their travels together—her husband's continued absence, and her own struggles with loneliness, childbirth, and parenthood—all in the context of an abiding faith.

In one segment of the journal, Dow reflects on their departure from her native America and arrival in Britain. "He gave me my choice, to go with him, or stay with friends in America, as there were many that told us I might stay with them. . . . But I chose to go and take my lot and share with him whatever might befall us. Consequently, on the 10th of November, 1805, we set sail from New York for Liverpool, in Old England. . . . Lorenzo came into the cabin, and told me to go on deck and bid farewell to my native land! I did so—

and the city began to disappear! I could discover the houses to grow smaller and smaller; and at last could see nothing but the chimneys and the tops of the houses. . . . In a short time nothing remained but a boundless ocean opening to view; and I had to depend upon nothing but the Providence of God! I went down into the cabin, and thought perhaps I should see my native land no more! The vessel being tossed to and fro on the waves, I began to feel very sick, and to reflect I was bound to a foreign land; and, supposing I should reach that country, I knew not what awaited me there. But this was my comfort, the same God presided in England that did in America!—I thought if I might find one real female friend, I would be satisfied."[8]

Place also involves the reality of geography, the movement from one place to another. In America and elsewhere, the terrain and geographical dimensions of the new place had great impact on the missionaries. Jacob Bower, Baptist home missionary, wrote in 1834: "The cause of Missions within range of my travels is not flattering. I have not been able to do much in the field for sometime back. The Cholera, that dreadful scourge, has visited Illinois; many towns have been almost evacuated. It was found necessary to suspend our preaching, except twice on Saturday and Sabbath."[9]

As an evangelical nomad, the frontier preacher, like his Lord, often had no place to lay his head. In fact, some within the Christian community were apparently suspicious of those preachers who desired material goods in even the most basic sense. Bower commented: "Some people love much in word and in tongue, but not in deed and in truth. They say, 'we like to hear you preach—we are fond of you—come and preach for us,' but only mention their duty,—that the labourer is worthy of his hire, and they will be offended, and say, money-hunter, beggar, missionary. . . . Under these circumstances, the poor missionary must wear out his clothes, his horse and saddle, his body, lungs, and voice, and spend his whole living, and get no help from those who pretend to love him so well. The things are very discouraging."[10]

Bower, like other traveler-preachers, details some of his

journeys, the movement from place to place, preaching, baptizing, and always on the move. "Since May 19, I have rode 372 miles, preached 42 sermons, and baptized one—and there are 4 hopeful converts—making in all since the date of my commission, 1247 miles, 191 sermons and 43 converts."[11] Yet, in time, the harsh places seemed to become more like home. In some of the most impossible and harshest of places, missionaries found the gospel taking hold. Again, Jacob Bower wrote in his journal February 24, 1834: "The good cause is evidently gaining ground, though its progress is slow; it is like the morning dawn; darkness imperceptibly withdraws, and the light approaches. Opposers are not so saucy and violent as they were two year ago: it will be a great work to get professors properly into their duty. In 81 days, I have ridden 634 miles, preached 75 times, baptized one, and aided in the ordination of one preacher. I have cheering prospects of communicating to you some good news in my next. I have sat down and wept with a mixture of sorrow and joy, when thinking over the distressing situation of Zion in Illinois, and how God has remembered her in mercy."[12]

These are fascinating accounts of the uniqueness, hardship, joy, and death that confronted missionaries as they moved to the places where they believed God had called them. Their language reflects the theology of the times, the struggle to come to terms with environments that were at once hopeful and threatening, and the necessity to search for God when children were born or when families were struck down in conflict.

The question of place is a riddle. Why do some people find a place—spiritually, personally, geographically, or theologically—and remain there while others move on from place to place in search of something else, willing to leave the safety of one place for the uncertainty of another? It is a mystery, true enough. For example, sometimes the symbols of place overlap in the missionary endeavor.

In his study of the Cherokees, William McLoughlin says that in spite of their cultural and racial diversity, Baptist missionaries and Native Americans shared an important place

together: the river, and the importance of water baptism. He
notes that the Baptist idea of total immersion as burial from
sin and a resurrection to new life was not lost on Native
Americans like the Cherokees. That tribe had a traditional
purification ceremony called Going to Water. McLoughlin
writes: "The Cherokees had always believed that rivers, like
fire, wind, sun, moon, and smoke, were of spiritual significance. They were a river people, and Going to Water was a
regular source of spiritual renewal to them. Thus the Baptist
movement struck another responsive chord in the traditional-
ist Cherokee."[13]

The ceremony of baptism with robes, singing, prayer, and
immersion helped bring together two unique religious places
for white missionaries and Native Americans alike.
McLoughlin observed that the baptismal ritual "was very sat-
isfying to those making the transition from the old religion to
the new, and it was employed by no other denomination" in
the Cherokee region.[14]

In a strange way, two traditions shared a common place
at the river. Missionaries sought to offer a traditional Cherokee
place new meaning that demonstrated the power of the
gospel and the heart of Christian identity.

Perhaps Cherokees and missionaries had opportunity to
discover another truth, one as old as the covenant with
Abraham, Isaac, and Jacob. It is this: no place guarantees
God's presence, but no place is immune from it either. We,
like Abraham before us, discover in our searching that wherever the place, God has been there all along. The good news
of Christ means that beyond who we are, or what we have
done, beyond where we have come from or where we are
going, there is a place for each of us.

We live by that risky faith that God is present with us even
when we do not know precisely where the road will take us,
even when it seems we cannot find the way. We learn from
Abraham and these early missionaries that we have a place in
Christ anywhere we may be, but we cannot stay any place
forever. Faith, therefore, is a place, but it is no place. For the
church of Jesus Christ, faith is the security of belonging to

Christ, to a people, and to a community.

Think of all the places where the faith of God's people has revealed itself: on the way to Canaan; on the way out of Egypt; the empty tomb, Golgotha, the place of a skull; the sea of Galilee; the road to Damascus; the backside of some desert; the back row of some church; the classroom; the sickroom; in the upper room. God shows up in the unexpected places, in the risky places when our calling is sure and certain, and when it is not clear at all.

Peggy Dow illustrates that reality. While she and her husband were attempting to minister far from home in the British Isles, she gave birth to a child. Her husband, Lorenzo, left her with friends in England while he went to preach in Ireland. The child died almost immediately and Peggy Dow writes of her sorrow—the dead infant, the absent husband, the place that was not her home. A "kind sister" brought her the news. "She told me my child was gone, to return no more to me! . . . I felt as one alone—my Lorenzo in Ireland—my child was gone to a happier clime! I strove to sink into the will of God; but the struggle was very severe, although I thought I could say, 'The Lord gave, and the Lord hath taken away, and blessed be the name of the Lord!' . . . They carried my sweet little Letitia, and consigned her to the tomb, there to rest until the last trump shall sound, and the body and spirit be re-united again: and then we shall see how glorious is immortality!"[15]

Peggy Dow's experience was duplicated in many missionary families. Places took on new meaning as children, spouses, and friends encountered separation, disease, and death. Peggy and Lorenzo Dow returned to America, leaving their daughter buried in another place to which Peggy would never return.

Faith then is the security of belonging and the insecurity of growth and change, danger and death. We move "from faith to faith," the Apostle Paul says, going on even when we cannot see the way, when we have no secure place. The vision of Abraham was surely no less real than that known by Peggy Dow and others, even in our own day. Abraham's calling is addressed to all who go out in God's name. The risk of place is the same call that came to Abraham who by faith, "obeyed when he was called out to a place which he was to receive as an inheritance; and he went out, not knowing where he was to go. By faith he sojourned in the land of promise, as in a foreign land, living in tents with Isaac and Jacob, heirs with him of the same promise. For he looked forward to the city which has foundations, whose builder and maker is God" (Heb. 11:8-10 RSV). The journey continues . . .

FOR DISCUSSION

1. How does the story of Abraham's journey illustrate the significance of *place?*
2. In light of the missionaries cited in this chapter, what role does *place* have in understanding the church's mission?
3. Based on this chapter, how did specific places impact the early missionaries and their efforts to communicate the gospel in different locales?
4. Do the women cited here have a particular understanding of the nature of *place?* Why?
5. What did you learn from Peggy Dow's journal and her own experience of the missionary calling?
6. How important is the issue of place in the journey of faith? Why?

The Risk of **5**ommunity

During the school year 1988-1989, our family served as Baptist Mission Service Corps volunteers in Fukuoka, Japan. I was a visiting professor of church history at the Seinan Gakuin University in Fukuoka, located in the southern most island of the country. My wife taught English in various schools in the region. The Seinan Gakuin University, a school with strong Baptist roots, has an outstanding reputation among private schools in Japan. Its student body numbers near 10,000 students. Teaching in Fukuoka was one of the most important experiences of my life. It was also a wonderful opportunity to encounter the diversity of Christian community in an Asian university context. We made new friends among faculty and students as well as in the Japanese churches.

Worship was particularly meaningful for our family. On Sunday mornings we would usually attend the Seinan Gakuin Baptist Church directly across from the university campus. Naturally, the service was completely in Japanese, so much of what was said was lost on our family. There were important ways in which we found ourselves a part of community, however . . . moments that transcend linguistic and cultural boundaries in any congregation. For one thing, we began to

make friendships at the university and the church. Japanese
Christians welcomed us and sought to make us feel at home.
In addition, worship drew us together as we shared common
symbols of Christian community that carried us beyond the
differences of language and custom. For example, sharing the
celebration of the Lord's Supper was a moment in which we
could all partake regardless of our linguistic and cultural differences. At such times, the depth of that profound symbol
created a timeless bond between us and our Japanese friends.

Although many of us did not speak the same language,
we could share in the Lord's Supper, uniting in the Word of
God, in an observance beyond words, sensing community
in Christ. When the church celebrated the baptism of new
Christians, I again felt the unity of persons in Christ. Baptism
was a reminder that we were all part of the body of Christ,
the church.

When the Seinan Gakuin Church observed a service of
baptism, it was a powerful event. The entire service
revolved around the ancient rite. Candidates for baptism
were asked to give a statement of their faith and describe a
bit of their life pilgrimage. After the baptism, they returned
to the congregation and were presented special gifts to
mark the occasion (gift-giving is a particularly important
Japanese custom). Throughout the ceremony, I was
touched by the way that timeless Christian symbol seemed
to draw us all together.

On one occasion I participated in a worship service at a
church on the outskirts of Fukuoka. The congregation met in
an upstairs room over a pub (a fact that the members often
joked about). Early in the service we sang many gospel
hymns with which I was familiar. (I learned enough Japanese
to be able to join in the hymns.) Later in the service the congregation rose and boisterously sang the Apostles' Creed, one
of the most ancient confessions of faith in Christ. Suddenly I
realized how that act linked all of us within the broadest
boundaries of historic the Christian tradition. Imagine! A community of Japanese Baptists singing one of the earliest hymns
of the church in the latter years of the twentieth century, in a

congregation gathered over a pub! In both the gospel hymns and the Apostles' Creed we were linked with Christians across the ages and around the world. In spite of our differences, we were joined by common confessions and common faith. How much more diverse, how much greater sense of community could we have experienced with each other?

Those moments drew us together and helped me feel a sense of community in a new place with new people. In that context with those Japanese brothers and sisters, I discovered a new dimension of community with the people of God.

Such community is not without its risks, especially for Japanese Christians. Many enter the church over the objections of family and friends. Sometimes they are even made to feel that they are not "good Japanese" because they have stepped outside the boundaries of traditional Japanese religion and its union of Shinto and Buddhist traditions. At worst, those who confess faith in Christ may be ostracized from their families (although that probably happens less today than in previous generations). At best, many families simply do not understand the newfound religious commitment that has occurred. It is a risk, pure and simple.

Likewise, Japanese Christians, like Christians around the world, struggle with the nature of community in the church. They, like all the rest of us, must learn to work together in the common task of the gospel, relating, interacting, communicating, disagreeing, and reconciling one with another.

The mission of the church is never simply an objective endeavor of going out and proclaiming the gospel in a vacuum. The gospel calls Christians to confront together the dynamics of community. It involves the interaction of persons and the development of community. It has been like that from the beginning.

The church's first missionaries immediately confronted the risk of community. Paul's letters were addressed almost entirely to specific communities of faith, often in response to particular problems that had developed regarding the nature of community and the relationship of persons in the church. Corinth was perhaps the most problematic of the churches in their struggle with community. Church members were divided over their favorite preacher and authority figure (I Cor. 1:10-17); there was specific and public sin in the church (I Cor. 5:1-5); and there was division over the nature of spiritual gifts I Cor. 12:1-31). These were only a few of the problems in that conflict-driven Christian community. (Much of it sounds strangely contemporary, doesn't it?)

To such a church Paul emphasized the significance of community among the people of God. It was a unity symbolized in the Lord's Supper. Thus he writes to the Corinthians and to us: "When we bless 'the cup of blessing,' is it not a means of sharing in the blood of Christ? When we break the bread, is it not a means of sharing in the body of Christ? Because there is one loaf, we, many as we are, are one body; for it is one loaf of which we all partake" (1 Cor. 10:16-17 NEB).

The second-century Christians echoed this sense of unity and community evident at the Lord's table. The *Didache*, compiled in the second century, contains this reading from the observance of the Lord's Supper: "As this bread that is broken was scattered upon the mountains, and gathered together, and became one, so let thy Church be gathered together from the ends of the earth into thy kingdom: for thine is the glory and the power through Jesus Christ for[ever]."[1] The bread, like the church, was a union of many elements brought together into one loaf and one body.

The first efforts at establishing mission agencies and boards were based on the nature of Christian community. Such community did not come easily for many individuals and churches, particularly in America. Many Americans held a deep mistrust for religious establishments and "hierarchies" that in Europe had represented oppression and an autocratic approach to church affairs. Still others, particularly among Baptists and others of the free church tradition, feared that mission boards would usurp the authority and autonomy of local congregations. Many were uncertain as to the biblical basis for establishing such boards and organizations. Funds were limited. The future was uncertain. Community—missionary organization—was a risk, yet some were willing to attempt such an endeavor.

Women joined together for the sake of the missionary imperative, creating new communities for prayer and financial support of missionaries. The Boston Female Society for Missionary Purposes was one such community. Mary Webb, the group's first secretary, voiced the challenge and the risk in an address given in 1812. Their work was a community united in prayer for those who had gone abroad to carry the gospel. In fact, some of the earliest forms of community-focused missions took the form of prayer meetings, especially among women. As Mary Webb described it, groups of women were encouraged "to set apart the first Monday afternoon of every month for special prayer; and likewise soliciting a correspondence with them [missionaries] by letter. It was with much trembling and diffidence, we took this public step; but from the success which has attended our feeble efforts, we have reason to believe we were directed to it by unerring wisdom."[2]

Webb observed that this general call for prayer had linked communities of women in common endeavor. Indeed, she said, "By this means we have come to the knowledge of societies and individuals, which before we did not know existed; and we trust we shall have increasing occasion to rejoice, that this channel of intercourse has been opened."

Webb knew that these gatherings might not be acceptable to some, especially those who believed that women were exceeding their "place" in the church, attempting to function in what was a divinely ordered male realm. No doubt she had experienced criticism that these female gatherings could foster attempts by women to minister in areas reserved for men. She anticipated certain criticisms, commenting: "We are aware, that by thus coming out, we lay ourselves open to the remarks of the enemies of religion; but believing the path of duty to be guarded on the right hand and on the left, we feel safe. Our object is not to render ourselves important, but, useful. We have no wish to go out of our province, nor do we undertake to become teachers in Israel; it is our pleasure to

see our brethren go before, and we are content to be permitted 'to glean after the reapers,' and follow with our earnest
prayers, their more extensive labours: this privilege we must
covet. We cannot be willing to remain in a state of neutrality
in a cause which demands so much zeal and activity; nor can
we feel satisfied with being made partakers of the grace of the
gospel ourselves, without desiring to be instrumental of con-
veying the knowledge of it to others."[3]

It seems strange now (or does it?) that the organization of
communities whose primary purpose was for prayer and
financial support for missions should produce controversy,
but they did. Women had to convince certain men that their
work was essential and not threatening to the missionary task.

Debates and dialogues continued among Baptists and
other Protestant traditions regarding the nature and possibilities for development of organizations that would promote
and support missions. Francis Wayland (1796-1865) illustrates
the Baptist dilemma over the relationships between local
churches and missionary agencies. On one hand, Wayland, a
highly respected Baptist leader, affirmed the importance of
Baptist unity and cooperation. On the other, he wanted to be
sure that missionary boards and denominational cooperation
did not threaten the autonomy of that most significant form
of Baptist community, the local congregation. Writing under a
pseudonym in 1824, he lauded the benefits of community as
a unified effort to fulfill the missionary calling of the church.
Using the name "Backus" (no doubt a reference to the earlier
patriarch Isaac Backus), Wayland wrote: "United we stand,
divided we fall. . . . It is the duty of each of us as individuals,
to do all in our power to promote the interests of the
Redeemer's kingdom. It is also our duty to do it collectively
as a branch of the general church of Christ. But to do this, we
must act in concert. We do not wish to bind the consciences
of our brethren. We do not want to abridge the liberties of
any individual church. These we hold sacred, and we always
shall hold them so; but we want them to assist us, and want
to assist them, in all the plans that they or we may devise for
promoting the salvation of our fellow men. . . We have one

Lord, one faith, one baptism. Why should we not unite all efforts together, and thus do our utmost to promote the cause of Christ in the United States, and throughout the world?"⁴

The initial efforts at organizing missionary societies involved the risk of community. Leaders like Francis Wayland sought to convince a constituency that they could, indeed should, work together in carrying out Christ's commission to go to the nations, preaching, teaching, and baptizing in Christ's name.

Yet the actions of Wayland and others also assured that the broader community would not undermine the foundation of Baptist life and cooperation, the local church. Mission societies were essential for accomplishing what individual churches could not, but the autonomy of the congregation was also essential. Maintaining both organizations was imperative but difficult. It was a risky effort, to say the least.

The early missionaries quickly learned that they were not merely reporting on data, or passing along information, however important that data might be. They encountered other human beings who responded to their message and to the missionaries themselves in a variety of ways. Missions, therefore, exists in community. It involves issues of communication, trust, mutual interaction, and yes, even friendship.

In the 1820s, when Thomas Roberts and Evan Jones began their work among the Cherokees at the Valley Towns station of Georgia, they were surprised at the positive reception they received. Cherokee leaders made it clear that they wanted education for their children through the mission school. As one Indian told the Baptists: "We want our children to learn English so that the white man cannot cheat us."⁵

Baptist missionary Thomas Roberts wrote of the Cherokee children in words that challenged many Anglo-Saxon caricatures: "They are kind, obedient, and industrious." He also noted that their "mental powers appear to be in no respect inferior to those of whites." Roberts used white children as the standard for comparison, however. He wrote of the Native American youth, "Though their skin is red or dark, I assure you, their mental powers are white—few white children can keep pace with them in learning."[6]

While these missionaries apparently found community among the Cherokees, they were the exception among whites in general. One Valley Towns missionary observed: "The White people are constantly opposing every effort to instruct the poor benighted Indians. The great objection urged by most people in these parts is the enmity of the old wars in which some of their friends have been killed by them [the Native Americans]."[7]

The risk of community also involves the risk of a new language. Missionaries have long struggled with the languages of indigenous peoples to whom they wished to minister. Language is not simply a means of communication. It is a symbol of community, a means to friendship, and a way to understand another culture. Language is at the heart of community. And, like other issues we have discussed here, language is a risk. It is difficult, it takes great amounts of time, and the possibility always exists that we may use it inappropriately.

Consider particularly the risk and energy involved in language study for the early nineteenth-century missionaries who worked in America and abroad. They had few language schools; seldom did they have extensive study before they went out. Rather, they were thrown into a culture and expected to learn language and customs as quickly as possible.

Early American missionaries to the Native Americans confronted particular difficulty since few, if any, of their languages had been written down. Evan Jones, outstanding missionary among the Cherokees was accustomed to Welsh, Latin, Greek, and Hebrew, yet the Cherokee tongue was highly problematic for him. It took Jones almost ten years to learn to use the Cherokee language sufficiently to preach in it. What a risk, to spend so much time in language study. What a reality—ministering among a people for almost a decade before you could preach in their language.

Likewise, there were few Native Americans who could serve as translators. Early in his ministry among the

Cherokees, Thomas Roberts commented, "The misfortune is they do not understand English and we have no good interpreter."[8]

Cherokee students were equally distressed by the problems involved in learning English. Roberts noted: "Some of the boys who have been here for a long time trying to learn English without understanding what they read, became discouraged, went away, and we see them no more. Others seem to hang on between hope and despair."[9]

The risk of community can be frustrating, as persons struggle to communicate and as the difficulties of language weigh heavily on us. Even knowledge of a language and the ability to speak does not necessarily mean that understanding—real communication—will also occur. That too is a risk.

In his ministry with the Cherokees, Evan Jones acknowledged the difficulty of relating the Christian gospel and its accompanying belief system to the culture and community of the Cherokees. In their efforts to communicate the gospel to persons born of another social and geographic environment, the missionaries had to learn to listen. Evan Jones was aware that Native American beliefs and practices, indeed, their entire way of understanding the world, made it difficult for them to appreciate basic Christian ideas. He observed that Cherokees often viewed "all we said as mere legendary tales in which Indians would have no sort of concern." He even described one Cherokee who knew English but "seemed quite ignorant of the depravity of his nature, though he has often heard the gospel." Ideas such as the need for salvation and the atoning death of Christ were difficult to communicate. Jones suggested that "in their dark, uninstructed state they seem to have no other fear of death than that which arises from the apprehension of the bodily pain with which it may be accompanied."[10] Again, missionaries were brought into contact with a unique community and they were forced to come to terms with it. Some did, others did not.

With time, numerous Cherokees became Christians, and Evan Jones enlisted many of them in the effort to convert others in their community. In his book, *Cherokees and*

Missionaries, 1789-1839, historian William McLoughlin comments that "starting from the proposition that a zealous heart was a more powerful instrument for God's work than any other attribute, Jones collected an ever-expanding team of Cherokee converts and exhorters to assist him in the work of spreading Christianity and combating heathenism."[11]

Again, missionaries learned that Cherokee culture held rhetoric and public speaking in high regard, so the preaching of the gospel, particularly by persons of their own tribe, drew great attention. Likewise, Christianity came at a time when Cherokee culture was itself in transition (largely due to the coming of increasing numbers of whites) and Christianity offered a new religion of hope, promise, and courage. These missionaries learned to listen to the culture and respond to it.

Such a response was common among many missionaries. While many sought to listen to the new cultures in which they found themselves, not all were able to respond to their societies in healthy, creative ways. Tarleton Perry Crawford (1821-1902), Southern Baptist missionary to China, illustrates the dilemma that faced missionaries in relating to community.

In Irwin T. Hyatt's *Our Ordered Lives Confess,* a study of Baptist mission work in China, there are two photographs of T. P. Crawford and his wife, Martha Foster Crawford. The first is of the Crawfords in their early years as missionaries, young, intense, and clothed in western dress. The second photo is of an older, almost elderly pair, no less intense but clad in Chinese clothing. Crawford sports a long white beard like that of otherwise Chinese elders. That second photograph was no accident; rather, it reflected the way in which the Crawfords adapted to the Chinese culture and community. On his way to China, Crawford suggested that he went out for three reasons. First was his "desire to please Christ." Second was his "sympathy for the perishing heathen, especially the female portion." Third was "a desire to labor in such a place, and in such a manner, that the influence of my example may continue to live and be productive of good, after my sufferings and toils on earth shall have ended."[12]

But Crawford's methods and idealism did not protect him

from the terrible complexity of taking the gospel to another culture. His personality conflicts with Chinese and missionaries also alienated him from community. Crawford's life was characterized by great conflict both with the Chinese and within his own missionary community. He ultimately broke with the Southern Baptist Foreign Mission Board. At his death in 1902, Crawford was a broken, bitter man. Hyatt wrote, "when the 'natives' failed to heed his words of life they were rejecting him personally, telling him he was not the divine agent he believed himself to be."[13]

Hyatt also notes that while the lack of large success was a "common missionary frustration," Crawford's attitude was carried to "a degree happily uncommon among most missionaries."[14] Crawford's tragic life was not normative among missionaries, but remains an example of the difficulties of the journey to community.

A more positive response to indigenous culture is articulated profoundly in the life and words of the Baptist missionary matriarch, Lottie Moon, and her response to Chinese society. In her early days in China, Moon wore standard Western dress, believing that an attempt to wear Chinese clothes was to pretend to understand a culture where westerners could never be fully assimilated. Over time, however, she became more comfortable with Chinese culture and her place in it. Her dress was increasingly more in the Chinese style. She insisted that new missionaries "must be men and women of absolute self-consecration, ready to come down and live among the natives, to wear the Chinese dress, and live in Chinese houses, rejoicing in the footsteps of him who 'though he was rich, yet for our sakes he became poor.' " She continued: "We do not ask people to come out to live in costly foreign style . . . [barely] touching the heathen world with the tips of their fingers but we ask them to come prepared to cast their lots with the natives."[15] Understanding, indeed, participation in the community, was an inescapable element of missionary commitment.

Obviously, such a response to new cultures and peoples has its risks. As Lottie Moon warned, it may create misunderstanding as some believe that missionaries are pretending to participate in a "foreign" culture. It also means that missionaries must be willing to make mistakes, to commit various cultural embarrassments. But it is worth the risk. It is an inescapable element of community.

Such a response to Chinese community had a decided influence on the way Lottie Moon understood her own relationships with Chinese people, Christian and non-Christian alike. A sense of community with the Chinese meant that she learned to speak differently of her Chinese friends. Caricatures had to go. She wrote to friends in America: "Isn't it time that we missionaries part company with those who roll this word heathen under their tongues as a sweet morsel of contempt? Shall we Christians at home or in mission fields be courteous in preaching the gladdest tidings on earth, or not?" Instead, she suggested, missionaries should "speak respectfully of non-Christian peoples."[16] Lottie Moon had learned a valuable lesson about the risk of identifying with a new community of persons and valuing them as human beings. Such community led her away from common stereotypes to an openness and love for those who received the gospel she declared and those who did not. All were individuals loved by God.

Moon's fascinating experiences in China reveal another element in the risk of community. Missionaries themselves must risk community in their relationships with one another. Gaining this community is not always easy. Consider these early nineteenth-century missionaries to China. Thrown into a new, diverse, and often antagonistic culture, they were constantly under the stress of their "foreignness," the language, the energy required to fulfill their calling and simply perform daily tasks in an unfamiliar environment. If deep friendships sustained (and they did), stressful moments brought strained relationships. When Lottie Moon arrived in the Southern Baptist mission in China in 1873, she discovered that the first generation of Southern Baptist missionaries were torn by hatreds and grudges. Southern Baptist missionaries to China in this period were a tough lot of seasoned individualists who maintained distinct ideas about the way in which they were to function for Christ in a foreign land. Disagreements surfaced over such questions as the use of church property and the leadership of the Baptist China mission. One missionary even suspected that another was involved in a Chinese plot to assassinate him!

Lottie Moon learned quickly that community is no easy matter. She worked hard to bring harmony to the missionary environment while making every effort not to be drawn into old disputes. It was a formidable challenge. It was part of the risk of community.

Wherever the location and whatever the method, the missionary calling involves an inescapable invitation to community. Missionaries, wherever they may be, must learn to listen to the people to whom they seek to minister. Missionary action involves a spoken witness, true enough, but we do not "talk at" others. Rather, we listen, we hear, and we care for those in our paths. We offer friendship to those who receive the gospel and to those who do not. Likewise, we are called to experience and cultivate community among our brothers and sisters in Christ. Christian community does not simply happen. It, too, must be cultivated. It is hard work.

Community among Christians is also risky business. However risky it may be, community is an inescapable element of Christianity. In fact, the way Paul tells it, Christians have no choice but to participate in the community of faith, since all are "grafted" into it through faith in Christ. He wrote to the Corinthians: "But God has combined the various parts of the body, giving special honour to the humbler parts, so that there might be no sense of division in the body, but that all its organs might feel the same concern for one another. If one organ suffers, they all suffer together. If one flourishes, they all rejoice together. Now you are Christ's body, and each of you a limb or organ of it" (I Cor 12: 24-27 NEB).

From its very beginning, Christian missions meant that Jews and Greeks—all races and cultures—had to learn to struggle with the call to community in all its blessings and its complications. Such lessons are difficult ones then and now.

But we have no choice if we are to claim our unity in Christ. If we belong to Christ, we belong to His body, the church. We belong to the community of faith, the people of God. Good news!

FOR DISCUSSION

1. Reflect on any experience of community you may have had that parallels the description of missions in Japan discussed at the beginning of this chapter.
2. Why did the early Baptists have reservations about organizing missions boards?
3. Based on this chapter, how did early missionaries understand the nature of Christian community? Was their approach appropriate? Is it appropriate for today?
4. What should be the attitude of missionaries toward cultures different from their own?
5. How does this chapter expand your understanding of the nature of Christian community in your particular cultural and religious context? Think of examples.

The Risk 6 of Ministry

On June 20, 1971, I was ordained to the gospel ministry, so the ordination certificate still reads. It was in Texas, of all places. I received ordination to the Christian ministry in the Northridge Baptist Church, Mesquite, Texas, on a hot summer Sunday afternoon. My church history professor, friend, and mentor, William R. Estep, drove the fifty miles from Southwestern Baptist Theological Seminary in Fort Worth to preach the ordination sermon. Like many other students, I held my professors in awe, and I was delighted that Dr. Estep had consented to participate in the service.

The ordaining council met before hand, and after questioning me on various topics such as God, the world, and other things, the members voted to recommend my ordination. The service itself was basic and to the point, like Dr. Estep's sermon. It was attended by friends and family, folks who had believed in me and affirmed me throughout my life. Frankly, I remember little of what was said, but I have profound memories of that unspoken ritual, the laying on of hands, a symbolic act that over the years has taken on greater, even sacramental, significance in my life. By sacramental I simply mean an "outward and visible sign of an inward and spiritual grace." Something of what happened that day has become a part of my own life and identity in ways that I cannot adequately express.

What I still celebrate is this: some people trusted God and the future enough to take a chance on me as a gospel minister. It was a risk then. It still is. Perhaps some of them hesitated, just a bit, even then. After all, I was a child of the 1960s and the fact that I quoted the Beatles along with Jesus in some of the few sermons I preached probably made some of those Texas Baptists a bit nervous. They took a chance on me, nonetheless.

When it was time for the laying on of hands, everybody participated who wished to do so—a bit of radical congregationalism in that Texas church. I remember the people trooping by—teenagers with whom I had worked as a youth minister, Sunday school folk, deacons, a stray preacher or two who dropped by, some of my relatives, and friends who helped raise me.

When it was over they had a reception, and then my wife, Candyce, and I got into our 1968 yellow Ford Mustang (the most wonderful car I ever owned) and set out for graduate work at Boston University. Since that day, many things have changed. The Northridge Baptist Church does not exist anymore. It merged with another congregation and changed its name.

What did my ordination that was more than two decades ago mean? Did it convey some supernatural authority by which other Christians are brought into submission? Not for a moment. Did I understand at the time what it meant and where it would take me? Not for a moment. Yet what they did that June afternoon continues to have a profound effect on me. It involves the risk of ministry.

So the Word of God comes to all those who are on mission in the world. "You are a chosen race, a royal priesthood, a dedicated nation, God's own people, to proclaim the triumphs of him who called you out of darkness and into his marvelous light. Once you were no people, now you were God's people; once outside his mercy, now you have received mercy" (1 Peter 2:9-10 NEB).

It is that realization—that I am a priest within a community of priests—that helps me confront the risk of ministry in what sometimes seems a dark and terrible time. The idea of the church as a priestly community, a community of ministers, is at the heart of the gospel message. The priesthood of all believers is one official Protestant description of that idea, but there are other ways to say it. We are priests, everyone of us, "Priests to each other," as Carlyle Marney used to say.[1] And he was right. Such an idea is risky, sure enough.

For Christians on mission in the world, the risk of ministry involves two powerful concepts. First, it means that all persons have direct access to God through faith in Jesus Christ without the need for any other human mediator. Second, it means that all Christians are called to be ministers and do ministry, caring for one another and sharing God's love in the world.

This idea is present throughout Scripture. The covenant with Israel involved a promise that the people of God would be "a kingdom of priests, and an holy nation" (Ex. 19:6 NEB). While there was a priestly class in Israel—the Levites, charged with particular religious functions—there is a sense in which the whole nation possessed a priestly calling. Through the life and witness of Abraham's children, all nations would be blessed (Gen. 12:1-3).

The early Christians declared that Christ Himself was the great high priest between God and humanity. Those who followed Christ were a "royal priesthood," God's new people, the church. As such, they could "approach the throne with boldness, so that [they] may receive mercy and find grace to help in time of need" (Heb 4:16 NRSV).

Likewise, the power to minister came from the Holy Spirit. At Pentecost, that power and calling fell on all who waited on the Spirit, male and female alike. Indeed, in explaining the outpouring of the Spirit, Peter recalled the words of the prophet Joel. "God says, 'This will happen in the last days: I will pour out upon everyone a portion of my spirit; and your sons and daughters shall prophesy; your young men shall see visions, and your old men shall dream dreams. Yes, I will endue even my slaves, both men and women, with a portion of my spirit, and they shall prophesy' " (Acts 2:17-19 NEB).

Such a calling to minister was dangerous from the beginning. Stephen, one of the participants in the dramatic Pentecost events, was also the first Christian martyr, struck down for daring to declare God's word to hostile hearers. The Apostle Paul was convinced of his calling as a minister and messenger of God. He recounted his conversion from persecutor to persecuted in several of his letters. Yet such a decision kept him on the run. Remember that early in his mission he had to be protected by the underground church, smuggled out of Damascus, over the wall in a basket, to escape arrest. Arrests were inescapable, however, and Paul saw the inside of many a Roman jail before he finally laid down his life for the risk of his calling. Throughout his missionary journeys he was set upon by mobs, beaten, shipwrecked, and even bitten by a poisonous snake. How did he explain it? He said his calling was to proclaim Christ—to know Christ and make him known.

The early Christian communities of the second and third centuries knew something of the risk of ministry. One of their major dilemmas involved the question of trust for all the traveling preachers who came around, each claiming to be a representative of Jesus Christ. Some were true ministers, offering insightful teaching, selfless love, and enduring service in the proclamation of the gospel. Others were not so well intentioned and, even that early in the church, division and strife had occurred over the teaching and morality of some who claimed to represent Christ.

In response to this dilemma of sorting out true ministers from false, the second-century church developed a fascinating and creative way of receiving preachers. The method is described in the treatise entitled, the *Didache,* or *The Teaching of the Twelve Apostles,* probably compiled around A.D. 110. It reads: "But let every apostle that cometh unto you be received as the Lord. And he shall stay one day, and, if need be, the next also, but, if he stay three, he is a false prophet. And, when the apostle goeth forth, let him take nothing save bread, till he reach his lodging, but if he asks for money, he is a false prophet."[2]

Thus Christians were admonished to receive all preachers innocently, as if they were sent by Christ Himself. But they only allowed such preachers to remain among them for a day or two, lest they disrupt the flock with questionable teaching. These early believers no doubt followed the admonition of their Lord to "be wary as serpents, innocent as doves" (Matt. 10:16 NEB). Are there lessons for us today?

This idea of the Christian's calling and its accompanying riskiness has significant implications for our understanding of missions. First, as Baptists have often said, it means that individuals can be trusted in matters of religion. Each individual is competent to relate directly to God for salvation and calling. Each individual can be trusted to interpret Scripture and calling according to the dictates of conscience and the guidance of the Holy Spirit. Each individual is free to live out such a calling without coercion of or interference from national government or ecclesiastical tribunal. The people can be trusted in matters of religion—that is a dangerous and risky idea.

Such radical freedom is risky. It demands radical responsibility. To say that we are free to come to Christ, free to interpret Scripture and calling, does it mean we are free to believe or do anything we wish? Those who accept God's gracious calling to witness and ministry, must live with the risk of wrong choices and sinful actions. They do not live to themselves but within the community of faith, the body of Christ, the church.

At the same time, the risk of our calling means that we are called to care for one another. For the early Christians, conversion, not ordination, made all Christians ministers. Paul acknowledges that each person has different gifts to be expressed within the community of faith, but all Christians were to demonstrate the gifts of the Spirit (Gal. 5). All Christians were to "bear one another's burdens, and in this way fulfill the law of Christ" (Gal. 6:2 NRSV). Jesus himself made no distinctions as to those who would fulfill the Great Commission. All are commanded to go into the world and make disciples of all the nations (Matt. 28:19-20).

The earliest Baptists in seventeenth- and eighteenth-century England were common folk who supported themselves as tailors, weavers, tinkers, soap makers, and brewers.[3] As we have noted, they dramatized their common calling in two great symbols: baptism and the laying on of hands.

Baptism was the great equalizer. It united persons of low and high estate in the bond of Christian love. By laying hands on the newly baptized, Baptists symbolized that every believer was called to ministry. All were to be ministers in the world.

All these responses to ministry are decidedly risky. The freedom to read Scripture for ourselves creates the possibility that we might not read it correctly. The calling to minister may mean that we do the wrong thing in the wrong way at the wrong time, and do more damage than good. The way in which we fulfill our individual callings may put us at odds with others in the Christian community creating animosity and conflict. Nonetheless, it is a chance we must take if we are to accept the gospel mandate to carry the story of Jesus to the world.

Missions compelled women to accept the risk of ministry. Today we often debate the role of women in ministry, as if that is a new and "modern" occurrence in the church. The truth is that women have responded to the challenge of ministry from the beginning. Women as well as men were among the earliest Christian martyrs, willing to lay down their lives as witnesses for their faith.

In the eighth century, an Englishwoman named Leoba, a nun, was asked by Boniface, the great missionary to Germany, to leave her homeland and go to Germany as a teacher and founder of a convent. She and five other women responded to this call; Leoba became one of the leading missionary teachers of the period.

Her biographer, Rudolf, writing in A.D. 836 described her thus: "Trained from infancy in the rudiments of grammar and the study of the other liberal arts, she tried by constant reflection to attain a perfect knowledge of divine things so that through the combination of her reading with her quick intelligence, by natural gifts and hard work, she became extremely learned."[4]

Yet her piety and spiritual maturity were as profound as her learning. She was, Rudolf said, "held in veneration by all who knew her." Even the bishops, the leaders of the medieval church, sought her insights, "because of her wide knowledge of the Scriptures and her prudence in counsel."[5]

Here we have the story of a little-known woman who risked ministry in a foreign land by teaching and living the gospel within the context of her times. How many more women in the Middle Ages, whose stories have never been told, responded to missions through a ministry of love and learning?

The risk of ministry is also evident in women who never left home, but whose lives were deeply committed to the ministry of the church. Mary Webb was such a woman. Webb (1779-1861), who was disabled and used a wheelchair, was the founder of the Female Society for Missionary Purposes. This organization, begun in October 1800, was formed by Baptist and Congregational women in Boston. Webb and the women who joined her were determined to promote the "diffusion of gospel light among the shades of darkness and superstition."[6] Women were encouraged to contribute two dollars a year to the society and engage in prayer for missions on the first Monday afternoon of every month. This was missions, combining limited resources in an effort to make known the gospel.

There were also women who felt called to missionary service and were willing to take the risk—a risk that began with the application process. As in the case of Ann Hasseltine Judson, married women were in the first wave of missionaries to leave America for service abroad. Appointment was more difficult for single women who felt the call to missionary service. Charlotte H. White was such a women.

In 1815 White, a widow, applied to the Baptist Board of Foreign Missions, asking for their appointment to Calcutta in the fulfillment of her calling to the mission field. She even offered to provide her own funding and to live with her sister and brother-in-law who were already in India.

Charlotte White's statement of her calling is a classic example of the risk of ministry in the life of this woman who sought to do mission work. It states: "The Board will naturally inquire into my motives and expectations. Permit me to represent them. It is now about ten years since I was led to search the Scriptures in order to find assurance that Jesus Christ is the son of God; in doing which, I was blessed with a desire to be converted from

darknes [sic] to light. . . . Since the date of my conversion, I
humbly hope my desire has been to do good, and glorify my
Redeemer: and especially since missionary endeavors have
come within my knowledge I have felt myself deeply interested
in them; and their success has been the constant subject of my
prayers. Hitherto I have been excluded from rendering any service to the mission; but I now rejoice that God has opened a
way, and directed my mind to missionary exertions. . . . Having
found no period of life exempt from trials, I do not expect to
leave them on leaving my native land, but rather to add to their
weight and number."[7]

White's words reflect a profound sense of calling and a willingness to risk hardships and trials, and, as she said, "to suffer
the hardships of such an undertaking" in the proclamation of
the gospel.

Other single women followed White to the mission field.
Betsey Stockton was the first unmarried "missionary" appointed
to a foreign land. Stockton, an African American, was sent to the
Sandwich Islands in 1823. A former slave, she was not officially
appointed by a mission board but worked in the house of a
white missionary. Educated, she also ran a school.

The first single female to be sent out as an "official" missionary was Cynthia Farrar. A Congregational missionary, she
was sent to the Marathi Mission in Bombay, India, in 1827.
The mission requested a single woman who could serve as a
teacher and give full time and energy to the endeavor. Farrar
served for 34 years.

The twentieth-century missiologist R. Pierce Beaver insists
that "American women rallied to the new cause of overseas missions with enthusiasm. In it they would soon find a role of ministry and status denied them in the churches in the homeland."[8]

Through these missionary journeys and organizations,
women took on themselves the risk of ministry. They challenged the churches to think of missions in concrete ways as
tangible as a few cents a week set aside for funding new ventures. They also offered their own lives in missionary service,
some along with their spouses, others alone.

These efforts sometimes met with opposition from male

leaders, clergy, and laity. Yet the women went on with it. They were claiming ministry for themselves.

In her book, *Great Women of the Faith,* historian Nancy Hardesty notes that "by 1900 there were ninety-four sending agencies and forty-three supporting ones. Of these, forty-one were women's boards. Major impetus (for these endeavors) came from the women's rights movements and its promotion of women's education."[9]

Women also accepted the challenge of ministry at home. Isabella Graham and her daughter, Joanna Graham Bethune were two women who established a ministry to the poor of New York City through the development of one of the earliest Sunday School programs in America. Nancy Hardesty reminds us that Isabella Graham had a long association with institutions and activities of Christian benevolence. In 1797, she helped organize the Society for the Relief of Poor Widows with Small Children. It was later called the New York Orphan Asylum.

Increasingly concerned about the spiritual and educational limitations of inner city children, Isabella and her daughter, Joanna Bethune, established their first Sunday School in 1803. The schools opened on Sunday morning for the benefit of poor children who were unable to afford schooling or who were employed in factories during the week. They often involved women from various denominations who offered their services to teach the children to read using Bible stories and other religious materials.

Hardesty notes that opposition to Sunday Schools came from certain clergy and churches convinced that they undermined the Sabbath by creating work for children. She writes that some believed that "such schools usurped the rights of parents and local churches, that interdenominational cooperation was dangerous, and that church buildings should not be used for the general education of non-members."[10]

Yet the women persisted. Hardesty recounts an occasion when Ann Rhees sought to found a Sunday School in the First Baptist Church, Philadelphia, Pennsylvania. Her pastor was unenthusiastic but relented, and said, "Well, my sisters, you can try it; blossoms are sweet and beautiful, even if they produce no fruit." A Massachusetts Baptist deacon worried at the Sunday School endeavor said, "These women will be in the pulpit next!"[11]

So successful were the efforts of Graham and Bethune that six years after the Sunday School began in New York City it had more than 600 teachers and almost 700 students. Joanna Bethune herself taught a Sunday School class until she was over the age of eighty.

As we consider the risk of ministry, especially as it relates to women and missions, it is important to remember the Indian missionary Ramabai, a woman not known to most western Christians. Ramabai (1858-1922) was born to a Hindu family in India. She married in 1880, and her husband died in less than two years, leaving her with a child. In 1883, while in England, she was converted to Christianity, largely through her reading of the New Testament and her contact with a community of Catholic sisters.

With conversion came a call to missions—the risk of ministry. In the sisters' love for impoverished women in England, Ramabai found a calling to the impoverished women of India. When the nuns read the story of Jesus and the Samaritan woman from John 4, she received Christ and His mission to women. Her realization was that "Christ was truly the Divine Saviour He claimed to be, and no one but He could transform and uplift the down-trodden womanhood of India and of every land."[12] Ramabai and her daughter, Manoramabai, were baptized into Christ, September 29, 1883.

Returning to India, funded by the Ramabai Society, an organization of English women, she began a school for girls (Indian "child-widows"). Christian and Hindu young women were received equally. Some became Christians, others did not. All were received and instructed in what Nancy Hardesty calls "basic and useful subjects."

When famine struck India—a frequent occurrence—Ramabai was quick to develop aid to women widowed as a result of the harsh conditions. Through it all, her educational work continued. Through her witness a revival broke out among Indian women. In 1901 some 1,200 girls came to faith in Christ. Concerned that such an awakening continue, Ramabai organized prayer groups. Hardesty writes, "There followed a great revival which paralleled in may ways the beginnings of Pentecostalism being experienced in America."[13]

Among other things, toward the end of her life, she learned Greek and Hebrew in order to translate the Bible into Marathi, one of the Indian dialects. She died April 5, 1922, still reading the galley proof for the Bible translation. Her Mukti Mission, which means "home of salvation," still carries out its mission in India.

Ramabai and the other women discussed here reveal that ministry is a risk. Yet their lives also reflect the calling of women to declare the gospel wherever the Spirit leads. Those who accept the risk of ministry must be willing to face the danger, the ridicule, and the misunderstanding that is inevitable. Such ministry also is stressful to a fault. It takes its toll on persons emotionally, physically, and spiritually. That too is dangerous. Thus, those who would seek to minister in Christ's name must seek growth and learning, patience and maturity in their response to others and to themselves. Ministry takes great energy, causes great stress, and sometimes involves substantial danger.

Likewise, ministries are often carried out by people we least expect. Many of the persons discussed here would not have appeared on the church's "next great minister list." Have you ever noticed that Jesus loved getting His listeners hooked into a story and then throwing in a ringer, a hero that shocked the daylights out of everybody? How many of His stories end with the tax collector, the Samaritan, man or woman with a shady past as the hero?

Many of the individuals cited here came to ministry in unexpected, nontraditional ways, often through the back door. Many of them were not ordained in any official sense of the term. But they were called, nonetheless. They took the risk of ministry even when it meant that criticism, misunderstanding, and resentment were visited on them.

In the Baptist ordination councils of my youth, one question almost always was asked of every candidate for the Christian ministry. It was this: "If you are not approved for ordination by this council, what will you do?" The anticipated answer went

something like this: "Why, I'd preach anyway!" Part of the sense
of calling is the gnawing reality that the calling must be fulfilled
whether officially recognized by any ecclesiastical body. These
days there is something to be said for that kind of determination. Many who risked being on mission for God were outside
the bounds of "respectable" ministry, but they did not fear to
respond to God's call. Ministry remains a risk for the individual
as well as for the community of faith.

How many of us have been "priested" by folks who for all
practical purposes were least expected minister-types in our little worlds? How many of us retain the memory of persons,
unexpected persons, who were there when we needed them,
persons who took the risk of ministry and carried through with
it, and we were the beneficiaries of their love and care? They
took a chance on ministry and in doing that, they took a chance
on us. You see, we all need a priest from time to time. Like the
man in the good Samaritan's path, we wind up in the ditch and
cannot help ourselves. We need somebody to come along with
bandages and ointment, hope and understanding, and get us on
our way again, staying with us until we can care for ourselves.
Let us say it again. All Christians are called to be ministers and
all Christians need to receive ministry from time to time. All of
us have received the laying on of hands, spiritually if not literally. The call to ministry, the risk of ministry, belongs to everyone of us. It really does. Amen.

FOR DISCUSSION

1. In what way is the priesthood of all believers important for
   understanding the church's mission?
2. What makes Christian ministry risky? Give at least five
   examples.
3. What is unique about the role of women in the mission of
   the church?
4. How is ministry risky for women, past and present?
5. What does the example of past missionary endeavors such
   as those cited here have to do with future approaches to
   missions?

The Risk of Sacrifice

O ne day in May, 1825, a cart of the usual variety bumped and thumped with the usual violence along the hot, dusty highway leading from Ava to Amarapoora. Under its shabby cover sat a motley group of travelers—two little Burmese girls, a Bengali servant, and an American woman with a baby in her arms. . . . At Amarapoora, their expected destination, a disappointment fell upon the band of travelers. The object of their journey was not yet attained, for lo, the prisoners who had yesterday been removed by stealth from the death prison at Ava were not to be found at Amarapoora. Only two hours before they had been sent on their way to a village four miles beyond."[1]

This passage from *Ann of Ava,* Ethel Daniels Hubbard's biography of Ann Hasseltine Judson, details the journey, literally and figuratively, that Adoniram and Ann Judson took from America to Burma and its environs. In this account, Ann Judson, missionary and mother, ill and caring for her newborn child Maria, journeyed in search of her husband Adoniram, jailed by the Burmese. Finding him sick and emaciated, Ann Judson determined to remain nearby, bringing him food and comfort in his trouble. As her own illness deepened, she continued to find ways to secure food and medicine for her husband and her daughter. Ann Judson's writings detail her suffering: "I now began to think the very afflictions of Job had come upon me. When in health, I could bear the various trials and vicissitudes through which I was called to pass. But to be confined with sickness and unable to assist those who were so dear to me, when in distress, was almost too much for me to bear, and had it not been for the consolations of religion, and an assured conviction that every additional trial was ordered by infinite love and mercy, I must have sunk under my accumulated sufferings."[2]

In these powerful words, Ann Hasseltine Judson wrote of the struggles she confronted as a missionary spouse and mother in Burma. In accepting the missionary call, she accepted the risk of sacrifice, taking a chance that she might face, not only the loss of home, family, and security, but unknown hardships in another country. With great courage, she made that new land her home.

Judson's accounts remind us that we should not romanticize the missionary calling. Rather, we must acknowledge that it was and remains at times a call from God that includes suffering, sacrifice, and even death. So it was with Ann Hasseltine Judson. No sooner was her husband released from incarceration than her sickness claimed her life, banishing her to an early grave. She rendered the ultimate sacrifice.

In a letter written in 1827 to his wife's mother, Adoniram Judson described his sorrow and sacrifice in the loss of his beloved Ann. Judson was away in Rangoon when his wife died, and he described his return home to their daughter, who was being cared for by fellow missionaries. "Amid the desolation that death has made, I take up my pen once more to address the mother of my beloved Ann. I am sitting in the house she built, in the room where she breathed her last, and at a window from which I see the tree that stands at the head of her grave, and the top of the 'small rude fence' which they have put up 'to protect it from incautious intrusion.' " When his daughter Maria "turned away from me in alarm," Judson was, in his words, "obliged to seek comfort elsewhere, [and] found my way to the grave. But who ever obtained comfort there? Thence I went to the house, in which I left her, and looked at the spot where we last knelt in prayer, and where we exchanged the parting kiss."[3]

Judson continues the letter with his own thoughts as to the meaning of Ann Judson's death, noting that, "the doctor is decidedly of opinion that the fatal termination of the fever is not to be ascribed to the localities of the new settlement, but chiefly to the weakness of her constitution, occasioned by the severe privations and long-protracted sufferings she endured at Ava. O, with what meekness and patience, and magnanimity, and Christian fortitude, she bore those sufferings!"[4]

Writing of the occasion, Judson confessed his sorrow at his wife's passing, while continuing to affirm his faith. He wrote that, "she has been torn from her husband's bleeding heart, and from her darling babe; but infinite wisdom and love have presided, as ever, in this most afflicting dispensation. Faith decides that it is all right, and the decision of faith eternity will soon confirm."[5]

Adoniram and Ann Judson confronted illness, imprisonment, and death as a result of their response to the call of God. They struggled with their situation in the new land, facing hardships together. They knew the call to sacrifice is at the heart of Christian missions. They were not alone. Across the years many persons on mission at home and abroad have known what Judson called "severe privations and long-protracted sufferings."

James Hudson Taylor was such a person. Taylor (1832-1905) was one of the best-known nineteenth-century missionaries to China. He founded the interdenominational China Inland Mission in 1865, and its programs of indigenous missions work became a model for other ministries. Taylor, a person of great insight and courage, spent much of his adult life in China. He made it home, yet he, too, met with pain, sorrow, and suffering, and he would not disguise those hurts with superficial piety. In the midst of his experiences he acknowledged his weaknesses and affirmed his faith.

In one letter to an American friend he describes an illness. "I have been very ill since I last wrote to you, through a severe attack of dysentery. My strength does not return rapidly. I feel

like a little child. . . . But with the weakness of a child I have
the rest of a child. I know my Father reigns: this meets all questions of every kind."[6] Taylor's faith sustained him in times of
physical pain and spiritual distress.

Often it was not disease but the natural elements of storm
and ocean that confronted the missionary with the inevitable
danger. The stories are too numerous to tell. In 1734, Moravian
missionary Gottlieb Israel left Germany for the Caribbean island
of St. Thomas. Not far from land, a shipwreck occurred and the
crew escaped in the only lifeboat. Israel and a Moravian colleague, along with several African Americans, sought escape
through the same rocks on which the ship had been wrecked.
Feder, the other Moravian, was tossed against the stones and
taken under. Israel was saved. A short time after his rescue, a
friend inquired of the Moravian missionary: "And what didst
thou then, when thou sawest thy brother drowned before thine
eyes?" His reply was this: "Then I sang the verse— 'Where are
ye, ye scholars of heavenly grace, Companions of the cross of
our Lord? Your hallowed pathway where may we trace, Be it at
home or abroad? Ye breakers of strongholds, where are ye
found? Rocks and dens, and the wild waste ground, The isles of
the heathen, the furious waves— These are from of old your
appointed graves.' "

The friend continued: "How was it with thee in thy soul?"

"I would have been the Lord's if I had died," Israel replied.
"The text for the day was quite clear to me: 'How the morning
star shines, full of grace and truth from the Lord.' "[7]

Perhaps there are no more eloquent statements regarding
the nature of sacrifice in missions than that found in the journal
of Harriet Winslow, nineteenth-century American missionary to
Ceylon, an island in the Indian Ocean. Winslow (1796-1833),
along with her husband, Miron, served as a Congregational
missionary until her death. Her journal and collected letters
trace her journey: early life, conversion, call to missions, and
life in Ceylon. Throughout the work, Winslow is brutally honest about the hardships of her journey, recounting the deaths
of several children among the struggles of life in a distant
land. Through it all she offers insight into the nature of the

spiritual life that sustained her in both joy and sorrow.

Prior to her departure for Ceylon, Winslow harbored few illusions as to the hardships and sacrifices ahead. She warned that some persons—specifically females—often romanticized the missionary experience, to their later detriment. Early in the journal she observed: "It is to be feared that, for want of such careful examination and prayer, some enter the path [to missions] . . . no longer new and untrodden by American females—without sufficiently considering whither it leads, or the spirit of self-denial which it requires. They go out, cheered perhaps by the smiles of friends, and encouraged by the approbation of all the churches, without reflecting that soon, amidst a people of strange speech, they will see these smiles only in remembrance, or hear the voice of encouragement only in dying whispers across the ocean; and that then, nothing but a thorough conviction of being in the path of duty, nothing but the approving smile of heaven can keep them from despondency."[8]

With surprising directness she declared her opinion that, "It is time that the romance of missions was done away. It has been of use, perhaps, in exciting attention to the subject; but no attraction from its novelty, no impulse from its moral dignity, will bear up and carry forward any one, amidst long-continued labors of almost uniform sameness, which, though dignified as to their object, and their connection with the conversion of the world, are yet, in nearly all their details, most humble and forbidding."[9]

Of the sacrifices of the missionary calling, Winslow wrote: "There are encouragements enough to any sacrifice—if what is done for Him who bought us with His own blood can be called a sacrifice—but, it must be from principle, and not mere impulse. Mere excitement will not answer. The mind must be kept steady; and there must be a willingness to take the more humble part of breaking up the fallow ground and casting in the seed, instead of gathering in the harvest, as well as some clear-sightedness of faith, to see in small beginnings germs of great and long increasing good. An ardent love for souls, and a deep sense of the constraining love of Christ, will support even a delicate female under any privation, and enable her to 'rejoice in tribulation also.' "[10]

Harriet Winslow's own experience of sacrifice is poignantly evident throughout the journal in various descriptions of the deaths of several of her own children. Her struggles with sorrow and faith reflect the truth of her warnings about romanticizing missions. I include only a few brief excerpts as illustration. In 1827, she wrote to a friend: "Our little George commenced his immortal existence on the 12th of May. Goodness and mercy have followed me ever since. How great a debtor . . . . May I trust in him [God] alone for myself and my children. Especially do I desire to consecrate this dear child, by faith to him. Oh my God, receive our little one; receive him as thine own. O let him have no other portion in time or in eternity."[11]

Even the supposed safety of America could not protect her children. In 1832, only five years after the death of one son, another, Charles, was taken, shortly after his return to the United States. She describes her pain at his leaving, a pain soon compounded by word of his death. "April 22, 1832. Near the close of the last year we were called to prepare our beloved son to go to America. Many a heart-rending pang did I experience; but I think I was graciously supported by Him who can do all things, and does visit the sinful also with His consolations. This trial was long contemplated, but never, till it was very near, did I expect to live to see it. I think I could scarcely bear another such. Charles' feelings were much exercised."[12]

"December 16. The Lord has come very near to us since I last wrote, and we have realized in part what was then so much dreaded. Dear Charles is no longer an inhabitant of earth; but is, I trust, before the throne of God and the Lamb. The shock was what few can conceive. Oh, how we loved him. How our expectations were raised concerning his usefulness. But the Lord has not seen as we see. He has cut him down, and, I doubt not, for the best and wisest reasons."[13]

By January 1833, Harriet Winslow herself was dead, apparently from a heart attack. Her husband, grief-stricken, wrote that her "mortal remains were deposited in the church [in Ceylon] near those of our dear [son] George; thus was one babe by the side, and one in the arms, of the fond mother; and the spirits of six are, I trust, with her before the throne. Oh! how she loved them; how she prayed for them; how assured she was of their final salvation. She was indeed a precious mother as well as wife and missionary." He added, "Our departed Harriet had for the last few months been fast ripening for heaven; especially since we heard of Charles' death. How severe was that stroke! But what rich blessings did it bring! It made her lean more entirely on her Saviour."[14] Winslow's life and memoir are highly instructive for understanding the risk that women took in venturing into missions. It is a costly calling.

Other missionaries faced the risk of sacrifice, less because of disease or distance than sheer persecution brought on by those who, for various reasons, rejected their faith and their presence. In his classic work, *A History of Christian Missions,* the late Anglican Bishop Stephen Neill recounted the story of persecution visited on nineteenth-century missionaries and other Christians in Madagascar. Much of the early missions work there was done by David Jones, sent out by the London Missionary Society in 1820. Jones himself had lost his wife and child in the course of his missionary journey. The king, Radama, permitted the missionary to work in Madagascar and numerous converts were made. A new monarch, Queen Ranavalona, instituted persecution against Christians beginning in 1835. Some two hundred Christians were put to death. When the persecution ended in 1861, it was said that "out of the recesses of the forests there came men and women who had been wanderers and outcasts for years. They reappeared as if risen from the dead. Some bore the scars of chains and fetters; some, worn almost to skeletons by prolonged sufferings from hunger or fever, could scarcely drag themselves along the roads that led to the capital. Their brethren from the city went out to meet them, and to help them, and . . . as they saw their old loved city again, they sang the pilgrim song: 'When the Lord turned again the captivity of Zion we were like them that dream.' "[15] The message brought by missionaries was the good news of Christ. Yet it was also dangerous news for many. In some cultures acceptance of the gospel created the potential for sacrifice among those who heard and believed. They were confronted with the possibility, indeed, the reality, of suffering, exile, and death. They, too, had to face the journey with courage.

The call to sacrifice is not limited to nineteenth-century missionaries, however. It has been heard by many of those who served Christ in the twentieth-century as well. Albert Schweitzer was perhaps one of the twentieth-century's most famous missionary-physicians.

Not all twentieth-century experiences of missionary sacrifice are as well known as those of Albert Schweitzer, one of the world's most renowned missionaries. Schweitzer was a person of multiple vocations and extraordinary talents. Born in Germany, he was trained in theology, music, and medicine, and performed brilliantly in each field. He wrote and taught in the field of theology and his book *The Quest of the Historical Jesus* was one of the most important theological works of the twentieth century. An accomplished organist, he gave concerts throughout Europe, all to great acclaim. A physician, he was trained in the best medical schools in Europe. With all these possibilities, Albert Schweitzer chose to become a medical missionary to Africa. In one of history's great ironies, that sacrificial decision made him more famous still. His mission, Lambarene, became an outpost of healing, as Schweitzer himself said, "on the edge of the primeval forest."

In his book *On the Edge of the Primeval Forest,* Schweitzer describes his decision to embark on a missionary journey. "I gave up my position of professor in the University of Strasbourg, my literary work, and my organ-playing, in order to go as a doctor to Equatorial Africa. How did that come about? I had read about the physical miseries of the natives in the virgin forests; I had heard about them from missionaries, and the more I thought about it the stranger it seemed to me that we Europeans trouble ourselves so little about the great humanitarian task which offers itself to us in far-off lands. The parable of Dives and Lazarus seemed to me to have been spoken directly to us! We are Dives, for, through the advances of medical science, we now know a great deal about disease and pain, and have innumerable means of fighting them: yet we take as a matter of course the incalculable advantages which this new wealth gives us! Out there in the colonies, however, sits wretched Lazarus . . . who suffers from illness and paine [sic] just as much as we do, nay, much more, and has absolutely no means of fighting them. And just as Dives sinned against the poor man at his gate because for want of thought he never put himself in his place and let his heart and conscience tell him what he ought to do, so do we sin against the poor man at our gate."[16]

Albert Schweitzer sacrificed multiple careers for the sake of the gospel. His caring, seminal mission work in Equatorial Africa provided healing for multitudes who came to Lambarene. There he practiced medicine, preached the gospel, prayed, and even played a special piano made with pedals like an organ. When the mission needed money, he toured European capitals, playing the organ and lecturing. His talents were not sacrificed, but utilized for the sake of the mission. The legacy of his sacrifice and his success has not been forgotten. Surely Schweitzer himself would have said that it was no sacrifice at all.

The conclusion of the book, *On the Edge of the Primeval Forest,* contains the following words. Written in 1920, their challenge remains. "Nevertheless, I have not lost courage. The misery I have seen gives me strength, and faith in my fellowman supports my confidence in the future. I do hope that I shall find a sufficient number of people who, because they themselves have been saved from physical suffering, will respond to requests on behalf of those who are in similar need. . . . I do hope that among the doctors of the world there will soon be several besides myself who will be sent out, here or there in the world, by 'the Fellowship of those who bear the Mark of Pain.' "[17]

Albert Schweitzer knew the call to risk life and reputation in the cause of Christ. He challenges us yet to respond to our world. But Schweitzer is not the only twentieth-century missionary who mirrors the risk of sacrifice. While most are not as famous as the renowned doctor, their experience of sacrifice for the sake of the gospel is no less real. Hugo and Ruth Culpepper are two such persons. The Culpeppers were missionary-teachers in China when the Japanese invaded that country. Arrested by the Japanese military, they were interned in a prison camp for the duration of the war, experiencing privation and sacrifice as prisoners of war. During the time, Dr. Culpepper gave himself to the study of the Greek New Testament, an experience he believes sustained him through the traumatic period.

I have know Ruth and Hugo for over twenty years. For much of that time we were colleagues on the faculty of Southern Baptist Theological Seminary in Louisville, Kentucky. I have heard Hugo speak about his prison camp experiences only on occasion. He does not present himself as a person who has made great sacrifice in the Christian journey. Rather, he tells about daily reading the New Testament in its original language as a source of spiritual strength and intellectual endeavor, even for a prisoner of war. Clearly, it was faith that carried them through those days of sacrifice and incarceration. Today the Culpeppers live in Waco, Texas, where their son Alan is a professor of religion at Baylor University. Their courage remains. They are twentieth-century examples of the risk of sacrifice in the service of God through Christian missions.

These excerpts from the lives and writings of the missionaries are instructive for several reasons. First, they detail the real life struggles of real people who chose to give their lives—literally—for the sake of a gospel calling. They reflect the risk of sacrifice that was, and remains, an undeniable element of the missionary life. For example, Harriet Winslow knew, even before she went out to Ceylon that there were hardships ahead. She could not anticipate, however, just how painful those hardships would be for her and her family.

Second, the missionary endeavor in a more "modern" world is no less a sacrifice, although the specifics of such sacrifice may be different. While it is true that many missionaries live quite comfortably in countries where medicine and other aspects of modernity provide certain security, it is also true that distance, separation, disease, and political unrest can create occasions of great sacrifice. Even with jet travel, distance remains a reality for missionary families. Children are often sent to boarding schools or return to the United States for education or employment. Such sacrifice is not lost on "missionary kids." As one daughter of missionary parents once told me, "At so many of my major life events, my parents were somewhere else, often on the other side of the world." That reality makes Harriet Winslow's warning about romanticizing the missionary life strangely relevant in the modern world. Missions is hard work, demanding a variety of sacrifices, physical, mental, emotional, and familial.

For example, innumerable crises in the missionaries' extended families is often compounded by distance, even with modern methods of travel and communication. Disease and illness can create complications for missionaries far away from home and family. Even with medical technology, missionaries still return from overseas responsibilities because of sickness. Those who go must know that they face the risk, indeed, the reality of sacrifice, in their calling.

Third, the materials cited here, largely from missionaries working outside the United States, illustrate that all ministry involves the risk of sacrifice. Jesus told his disciples, "If any want to become my followers, let them deny themselves and take up their cross and follow me" (Matt. 16:24 NRSV). No persons who take seriously the words of Jesus can suppose that he or she will be immune from sacrifice, suffering, and danger wherever they may be.

The call to a life of sacrifice is intricate to the gospel life. To tell the story of faith is to tell of the sacrifices experienced by God's people. The writer of the Book of Hebrews sang the song of such faith, writing of those heroes whose sacrifices were signposts of encouragement on the journey: "Need I say more? Time is too short for me to tell the stories of Gideon, Barak, Samson, and Jephthah, of David and Samuel and the prophets. Through faith they overthrew kingdoms, established justice, saw God's promises fulfilled. They muzzled ravening lions, quenched the fury of fire, escaped death by the sword. Their weakness was turned to strength, they grew powerful in war, they put foreign armies to rout. Women received back their dead raised to life. Others were tortured to death, disdaining release, to win a better resurrection. Others, again, had to face jeers and flogging, even fetters and prison bars. They were stoned, they were sawn in two, they were put to the sword, they went about dressed in skins of sheep or goats, in poverty,

distress, and misery. They were too good for a world like this"
(Heb. 11:32-38 NEB).

Why such sacrifice? Why this calling to risk life and limb in
Christ's name? The writer of Hebrews responds to such questions. "And what of ourselves? With all these witnesses to faith
around us like a cloud, we must throw off every encumbrance,
every sin to which we cling, and run with resolution the race
for which we are entered, our eyes fixed on Jesus, on whom
faith depends from start to finish: Jesus who, for the sake of the
joy that lay ahead of him, endured the cross, making light of its
disgrace, and has taken his seat at the right hand of the throne
of God" (Heb. 12:1-2 NEB). Sacrifice is the nature of Christianity
because Jesus, the center of the faith, personifies sacrifice and
self-giving love.

Thus the call to sacrifice continues for those who would
claim Christ's mission in the world. It is a legacy captured by
Anglican missionary Johann Ludwig Krapf (1810-1856). In 1844,
at the death of his wife and only son, he wrote these words: "Tell
our friends that in a lonely grave on the African coast there rests
a member of the Mission. This is a sign that they have begun the
struggle with this part of the world; and since the victories of the
Church lead over the graves of many of her members, they may
be the more convinced that the hour is approaching when you
will be called to convert Africa, beginning from the East Coast."[18]
Those words lead us to ask again, with the writer of the book of
Hebrews, "And what of ourselves?"

FOR DISCUSSION

1. Is sacrifice an inescapable element of the church's mission?
   Why?
2. Does the fear of sacrifice keep persons from missions? Why?
3. Harriet Winslow illustrates several issues related to the risk of
   sacrifice. What are they?
4. What do you think was Albert Schweitzer's greatest achieve-
   ment? What was his greatest sacrifice?
5. What is the nature of sacrifice for contemporary missions? Are
   such sacrifices different than those in the past?

The Risk of Conscience

They were exiles, those first Baptists in the New World, the scourge of "Christian" America. Roger Williams personified their plight. In 1636, the Puritan representatives of a "Christian Commonwealth" threw Williams, the eternal dissenter, out of civilized Massachusetts and into the forests of New England. In exile, he was "denied the common air to breathe in, and a civil cohabitation upon the same common earth; yea and also without mercy and human compassion, exposed to winter miseries in a howling wilderness." For 14 weeks he wandered, not knowing "what bread or bed did mean." The Narragansett Indians saved him, and he bought land from them to found Providence Plantation, and, by 1638, the First Baptist Church in America.[1]

Of Rhode Island and its religious radicalism, Williams wrote, "I desired it might be for a shelter for persons distressed for conscience. I then considering the condition of divers of my distressed countrymen, I communicated my said purchase unto my loving friends . . . who then desired to take shelter here with me."[2]

It was a colony, a church born in exile. It was a community born of the risk of conscience. Rhode Island became a sanctuary for seventeenth-century religious fanatics, holy rollers, and assorted theological weirdos (or so it seemed to the Puritans). As one Puritan preacher declared, "All Familists, Antinomians, Anabaptists and other Enthusiasts, shall have free liberty to keep away from us . . . the sooner the better."[3]

Missions, ministry, faith, indeed, the foundation of Christianity itself, involves the risk of conscience. There are times when conscience requires persons to respond to church and state, family and friends, work and community in ways that lead to controversy, dissent, and difficulty. Conscience involves that sense of truth, integrity, and justice that is non-negotiable, a willingness to stand for what is right even when it involves danger.

Conscience is a risk, pure and simple. It may lead an individual to "buck the system," to confront the religious, political, or community establishments. It may thrust a person into a minority position against the prevailing majority opinion. To stand for conscience's sake is to take a chance that one's views are true and trustworthy. It is a great risk to take. From the beginnings of the Christian church, the question of conscience has been a significant issue for those who would live according to the gospel.

Consider the early church's missionary endeavor. Soon after the powerful experience of Pentecost, the Apostle Peter had a powerful dream in which he was instructed to kill and eat animals considered to be unclean by Jewish religious regulations. When Peter refused, he received God's word: " 'What God has cleansed, you must not call common' " (Acts 10:15 RSV). Peter's vision was expanded from that dream to an understanding that even the despised Gentiles could receive the good news of Jesus. Yet the Scripture reminds us that old prejudices die hard, even for an apostle. Paul's letter to the Galatians tells us that in his mission to that Gentile city, Peter ate with the Gentiles until "certain men came from James," and the Jewish church in Jerusalem. Then Peter "drew back and separated himself, fearing the circumcision party" (Gal. 2:12 RSV).

Paul's response to Peter's racism reveals the power of conscience in the earliest missionary endeavors. His words are those of a man acting according to the dictates of conscience, the guidance of a higher law. Paul wrote, "But when I saw that they were not straightforward about the truth of the gospel, I said to Cephas [Peter] before them all, 'If you, though a Jew, live like a Gentile and not like a Jew, how can you compel the Gentiles to live like Jews?' " (Gal. 2:14 RSV). So intense was Paul's sense of conscience in this matter that he "opposed [Peter] to his face, because he [Peter] stood condemned" (Gal 2:11 RSV).

In the midst of missionary activity, preaching the gospel to the Gentiles, Paul's conscience would not allow him to remain silent while another Christian (who should have known better) offended Gentile brothers and sisters and undermined the universality of the gospel. Paul was willing to "go public" in his confrontation with Peter for the sake of the integrity of the gospel.

While all Christians are called to live according to the dictates of conscience and the leadership of the Holy Spirit, there may be specific occasions when, for the sake of the gospel, conscience is put to the test.

The early Christians often were compelled to stand for conscience in their own faith, refusing to worship false gods of Roman emperor or state. Many lost their possessions, went to prison, or suffered martyrdom.

William O. Carver, the great missiologist and longtime professor at Southern Baptist Theological Seminary, Louisville, Kentucky, observed, "Martyrdom was also a means of missionary extension, taking the term in all its meaning from simple witnessing without hindrance, through all the stages of opposition and persecution to the death of the witnesses for their testimony."[4] Their convictions, their commitment to Christ, and the power of their consciences would not let large numbers of first-century Christians deny the faith.

So it was with Roger Williams. Williams (1603-1683) came to the Massachusetts colony in 1636 as a teacher for one of the Puritan churches in the Boston area. A religious genius, he was one of those persons for whom conscience and the faithful adherence to conviction was everything. Roger Williams spoke his mind. This did not always make for friendly relations with the prevailing religious or political establishment of the new colonies. In fact, Williams was a royal pain in the religious establishment of New England from the moment he arrived. No sooner had he gotten off the boat than he was disseminating certain "erroneous and dangerous" opinions. For one thing, he said that the Native Americans, not the English king, were the sole owners of the American land and should be justly compensated for it. Williams himself spent much time in conversation with and ministry to the Native Americans. He was, in fact, one of the earliest American missionaries to the Indians. His book, *A Key to the Language of America,* was one of the earliest studies of Indian language published in the New World. He used this work to translate portions of the Scripture into the language of the Native Americans.

In addition to his support of Native American rights, Williams got in more trouble with Puritan authorities for suggesting that the authority of civil magistrates extended only to bodies and goods, not to souls and salvation—that civil government had "no control over human conscience." Williams's belief that civil government had no authority over religion or churches was a radical shift in political and religious thinking in his day. Most Puritan divines believed that without an official Christian religious establishment, theological chaos and moral anarchy would prevail. To protect this establishment they were willing to prosecute those who disagreed with them, hence the decision to exile Roger Williams from the Massachusetts colony.

Williams wrote often about the role of conscience in human lives. He called it "a persuasion fixed in the mind and heart of man, which enforceth him to judge (as Paul said of himself a persecutor) and to do so and so with respect to God, His worship. This conscience is found in all mankind, more or less: in Jews, Turks, Papists, Protestants, pagans."[5] To those who believed that the sword of state must be used to promote the church of Christ, Williams wrote: " 'tis impossible for any man or men to maintain their Christ by their sword and to worship a true Christ, to fight against all consciences opposite to theirs, and not to fight against God . . . ."[6] God would take care of His own, not through power and might but by the Spirit.

Where did Roger Williams and the early Baptists get such views? Did they come from secular humanism or religious fanaticism? Hardly. Theirs was not so much a faith for radicals as it was a radical faith, a faith that led them to pursue belief and missions even when it got them into trouble. It was a faith at its best in exile. It was faith that risked the journey to jail, poverty, and homelessness for the sake of conscience.

Williams was not the only colonial dissenter who was willing to risk life and limb for the sake of missions and conscience. Women also stood for conscience against the religious and political establishment. Mary Dyer was a Quaker missionary who came to Massachusetts from London in 1635. As friends of Roger Williams, Mary and her husband William returned to England with him to help secure a charter for the colony of Rhode Island. There they became Quakers, accepting the beliefs of the Society of Friends. These included the belief that the Inner Light of Christ was present in each person and had only to be awakened by faith; the idea that worship was found in silent response of the heart rather than elaborate rituals and services; and the concern to reach out to the most broken and rejected persons in society with the overpowering love of Christ.

Returning to America, she began to proclaim Quaker beliefs and was immediately arrested and imprisoned. Puritans refused to allow Mary Dyer to preach and exiled her to Rhode Island. Returning to Massachusetts, she continued to preach as a Quaker. Finally, in 1660 she was arrested and sentenced to death for violating certain laws against "the cursed sect of Quakers." Authorities urged her to repent of her Quaker ideas. She refused, saying, "Nay, I cannot, for in Obedience to the Will of the Lord I came, and in his Will I abide faithful to death."[7]

When they could not dissuade her, Mary Dyer was hanged as a heretic on Boston Common, June 1, 1660. The risk of conscience led to the first execution of a woman in the American colonies—a woman who was preaching the gospel as a Quaker missionary.

Dyer's words to her accusers also reflect the risk of conscience and faith in the face of imminent death. They are the words of a missionary certain of her calling and bound by her conscience. In an address to the General Court of Boston, Dyer declared: "Whereas I am by many charged with the Guiltiness of my own Blood; if you mean, in my coming to Boston, I am therein clear, and justified by the Lord, in whose Will I came, who will require my Blood of you, be sure, who have made a Law to take away the Lives of the Innocent Servants of God, if they come among you, who are called by you, *Cursed Quakers;* altho' I say, and am a living Witness for them and the Lord, that he hath Blessed them, and sent them unto you: Therefore be not found Fighters against God, but let my Counsel and Request be accepted with you, To Repeal all such Laws, that the Truth and Servants of the Lord may have free Passage among you. . . . "[8]

Mary Dyer was a Christian missionary who risked her life, as she herself said, for the sake of "the Light of Christ." Even her executioners, the enlightened defenders of the "Christian Commonwealth" of New England, could not put out the Light she proclaimed.

Baptist women also accepted the risk of conscience for the sake of their mission in the New World. In the 1740s an elderly Massachusetts Baptist woman named Esther White was jailed for refusing to pay an eight pence tax for support of the local Congregational (Puritan) minister. When her pastor, the renowned Baptist Isaac Backus, visited her in jail she reported, "that the first night she was in there she lay on the naked floor and she said she never imagined that the floor was so easy to lie upon before . . . and she said that she [would sit] there as long as God saw best she should." Although she could have been released by simply paying the tax, White remained in prison for 13 months. She was released only after the authorities became so embarrassed they could no longer hold her. She never paid the tax. During her imprisonment, her fellow Baptists visited her often, joining in prayers and hymns to encourage her in her witness.[9]

It is important to understand something here. These early dissenters saw their action for the sake of conscience as inseparable from their mission as Christian believers. To dissent was to be on mission in Christ's name. It was the expression—at least one expression—of their witness to the world and to the rest of the church. It was their mission to serve as witnesses to the liberation—the radical liberation—that was available to those who belonged to Christ.

In their efforts, Baptists were highly pragmatic. Historian William McLoughlin says that where the colonial Baptists were concerned, their resistance and dissent took many forms. Some wrote petitions addressed to their communities, articulately stating their views on religious freedom. Some went so far as to bring lawsuits against tax collectors, and town governments, challenging their right to tax matters of religion. Others organized grievance committees or lobbying groups to work in behalf of their cause. Still others wrote protests to the colonial governors and even the English monarch.[10] They saw these activities not simply as a political effort, but as a witness inseparable from their mission in the world.

Such a risk of conscience was not without danger. In 1778, in the town of Pepperell, Massachusetts, a mob armed with clubs, whips, and poles attacked a group of Baptists gathered at a nearby river for preaching and baptism. The Baptists were not breaking the law. Their views and their very existence was an occasion for religious bigotry by those who saw their dissenting positions on government and faith as seditious and a threat to the civil and religious order. Once again, this punitive response was instigated when the traveling Baptist preacher came to town, fulfilling his mission, proclaiming the gospel, calling sinners to faith in Christ and baptism into His church by immersion baptism. Conscience led them to risk personal safety to declare their message.[11]

These early colonial dissenters—Baptists, Quakers, and others—were a radical lot. They were a people who had been touched by a powerful, life-transforming experience of God's grace, and they were willing to sacrifice themselves for the ideas and convictions born of that grace.

And the American Revolution came and went; the Constitution with its Bill of Rights was secured. Suddenly Baptists awakened in the mid-nineteenth century to discover that life had changed; they had become the second largest Protestant denomination in America. (The Methodists were the largest.) The remnant had become a majority; the exiles had become something of an establishment, especially in the South where their numbers flourished.

Suddenly Baptists confronted a new challenge to conscience—the issue of human slavery. A people who defended the liberty of the human conscience were torn apart over the liberty of human beings. Some even developed biblical arguments for the defense of slavery. Richard Furman, first president of the Baptist Missionary Society (Triennial Convention) wrote one of the most famous defenses of slavery, the South's "Peculiar Institution." He declared that "the right of holding slaves is clearly established in the Holy Scriptures, both by precept and example." He insisted that, "had the holding of slaves been a moral evil, it cannot be supposed that the inspired apostles, who feared not the faces of men . . . would have tolerated it, for a moment, in the Christian church."[12]

Consciences clashed when other Baptists insisted that the Christ's admonition to "love your neighbor as yourself" offered a simple teaching that struck at the foundation of slavery itself. Ironically, many who advocated the church's missionary responsibility, also defended the enslavement of other human beings on the authority of Holy Scripture. Nineteenth-century Baptists and other Southern Christians generally agreed that slaves should be evangelized; most insisted that salvation changed only the slaves' heavenly status, not their earthly condition. But try as they might, they could not keep the full gospel from finding its way into the hearts and hopes of the slaves. Conversion brought liberation and conviction of conscience, even to those who were kept in bondage.

Thus in 1807, a Kentucky slave belonging to Miss Esther Boulware was disciplined by the Forks of Elkhorn Baptist Church where she and her mistress were members. She was charged with saying publically that "she once thought it her duty to serve her master and mistress but since the Lord had converted her, she had never believed that any Christian [could keep] Negroes or slaves." She got into even more trouble for declaring she believed "there was thousands of white people wallowing in Hell for their treatment of Negroes, and she did not care if there was many more."[13] That woman talked free, didn't she, even when she was classified as a slave? Such a willingness to risk for the sake of freedom and conscience was not born of politics or economics, but of the liberating power of Christ's gospel.

Liberation was the hallmark of the life of Harriet Tubman, one of anti-slavery's greatest advocates. Her mission was to bring slaves out of bondage, and she was willing to risk her life for it. Tubman (1820?-1913) escaped slavery in 1849, but her conscience would not let her remain in safety while others remained enslaved.

Thus she began her famous forays into the South, leading other black men and women along the Underground Railroad to freedom. Convinced that God was the author of her freedom, she also believed that God sent a guardian angel to protect her on her marches into and out of the

South. She made 19 trips into the South and brought over
300 slaves to freedom. Her own words on the subject
demonstrate the depth of her conscience and her willingness to risk. "I had reasoned dis out in my mind," she said,
"there was one or two things I had a *right* to, liberty or
death; if I could not have one, I would have the other; for
no man should take me alive; I should fight for my liberty
as long as my strength lasted, and when de time come for
me to go, de Lord would let dem take me." It was a mission she could not deny.[14]

It was that kind of liberation that gripped the consciences of African-American Christians in the twentieth
century, leading them to work for equal rights beyond seg-
regation. Is it correct to consider the Civil Rights activities
of African-American Christians a part of the church's mission in the world? In fact, the Civil Rights movement itself
began in the African-American churches—churches such as
Dexter Avenue Baptist Church, Montgomery, Alabama, and
Ebenezer Baptist Church, Atlanta, Georgia. Many of the
individuals who participated in the Montgomery bus boy-
cott of 1955, the action that marked the beginning of the
end of segregated facilities in the South, were active members of African-American churches. No one could convince
them then (or now) that they were not on God's mission
of liberation. They walked to work and walked to church
rather than support segregated public transportation. Some
lost their jobs, many faced angry mobs. In that sense they
accepted the risk of conscience for a higher cause.

When I visit the Civil Rights Institute in downtown
Birmingham, Alabama, I am struck by the centrality of the
churches' role in the movement for human rights. As the
photos, recordings, and other displays indicate, during
those years of turmoil and confrontation, people moved
from Christian worship to public demonstration. They
faced fire hoses, attack dogs, jail, and even death for the
sake of conscience. Across the street from the Institute is
the Sixteenth Street Baptist Church, the scene of the 1963
bombing that took the lives of four young girls. The

racially motivated terrorist activity occurred during Sunday School hour at the church. It galvanized public attention around the world and remains a powerful reminder of the price of conscience. That church, the point of origin for many marches and demonstrations in the name of liberty, remains a symbol of the risk of conscience and the cost of liberation. Its members continue to address the needs of persons, whatever their race, in inner–city Birmingham and throughout the community. They were and remain champions of liberation, willing to risk for the sake of conscience.

The risk of conscience also sent women on a mission to urban America. During the nineteenth century, many Christian women accepted God's call to respond to the overwhelming poverty of urban slums. In Christ's name they sought to confront the serious social problems of their generation, even when it brought criticism, rebuke, and danger. They were committed individuals whose consciences compelled them to respond to the social needs of the day. These women were active in temperance movements, prison reform, and efforts to care for the disabled, the illiterate, and the impoverished.

One such reform-minded woman was Margaret Prior (1773-1842), the first missionary funded by the New York Female Moral Reform Society, 1837. A friend said of her: "Her whole life was regulated upon the principle, 'Ye are not your own, ye are bought with a price; therefore, glorify God in you body and in your spirit, which are his.' " Prior's benevolence, her active, laborious, untiring, disinterested efforts to do good, were what particularly distinguished her. She lived not for herself, but to relieve human misery, and win souls to Christ. The world was her field of labor, and every son and daughter of Adam shared in her sympathies."[15] In short, Margaret Prior was driven by her conscience, a sense of destiny that would not let her rest, in the fight against hunger, poverty, and lostness.

Prior's conscience was particularly touched by the plight of young women who occupied the brothels of New

York City. As part of her famous "walks of usefulness"
through New York's slums, she sought to bring these
women out of a life of prostitution. Like other women
working in the slums, Prior also discovered that many
prostitutes were victims of a social situation that so
defined their status as to make them "social outcasts,"
and offer few opportunities for escape from their lifestyle
once it was underway. She spoke out against the social
and political system that often ignored the circumstances
in which the women found themselves.

She chastened a "heartless world" that, "when
requested to consider them, [the prostitutes] and inquire
for the cause and the remedy, turn coldly from us, and
perhaps treat our solicitude with derision: and the pro-
fessed Christian too, when desired by a fellow Christian
to feel and act, throws out some stale objection (in common use with the libertine) against the cause of purity. .
. . The men, too, who make the laws, and those commissioned to enforce them, think the subject so very delicate, that when they know there are fifty houses in a
single block, whose inmates, aided by agents in every
portion of the city, are constantly laboring, with all the
assiduity of demons, to destroy, do nothing effectual to
disturb them, especially if they are careful to keep very
still. No matter how many heart broken fathers, and
mothers, and sisters, are sent in sorrow to the grave by
their instrumentality. 'This is the land of liberty,' say they,
'and it is a question with us, whether anything can be
done.' If the public indignation were aroused as it should
be, and a correct public sentiment prevailed, methinks
the question would soon be settled."[16]

Margaret Prior demonstrated the risk of conscience in
the slums of New York. She acted in Christ's name to
bring specific individuals out of bondage to sin and hor-
rible circumstances. Yet she would not remain silent
about the conditions that contributed to those circumstances. She called church and society to respond to individuals and to corporate elements. As one of her friends

noted, she was a missionary "remarkable for devising ways and means of usefulness; her mind was fruitful in expedients."[17]

Prior and other reformers were often criticized for involving themselves in causes outside the domain of decent women. They often had to defend themselves, particularly for their public role and their outspoken criticism of the system.

Eliza Daniel "Mother" Stewart (1816–1908) was another of the nineteenth-century women who considered themselves missionaries to the oppressed. She was particularly active in the temperance crusade, sensitive to the way in which alcohol abuse impacted child and spouse abuse, poverty, and unemployment. When criticized for her actions in the public arena she responded: "It had been with many, a fearful struggle to yield up their preconceived ideas of what was a lady's place, and what the world might think and say. Not a few [women] carried the subject to their closets, and there on their knees fought the battle with self and pride before the Lord, till He gave them strength and they came forth anointed for the war [against alcohol]."[18]

So conscience shaped the missionary task from the beginning. Conscience and the exercise thereof is a dangerous thing. But it is the imperative of those who have been captured by the gospel of Christ. Missions is inseparable from conscience—the willingness to speak up and act in ways that bring help and healing to persons as well as judgment on the present evil age.

Mary Ann "Mother" Bickerdyke (1817–1901) said it well. Bickerdyke, a volunteer nurse in the Northwestern Sanitary Commission during the Civil War, was known for her work in caring for wounded soldiers—not without controversy. On one occasion a surgeon challenged her: " 'Madam, you seem to combine in yourself a sick-diet kitchen and a medical staff. May I inquire under whose authority you are working?' Without pausing in her work, she answered him, 'I have received my authority from

the Lord God Almighty; have you anything that ranks
higher than that?' "[19]
    Conscience, thank God, conscience!

FOR DISCUSSION

1. What is conscience? How would you define it?
2. What do the colonial Baptists teach us about the role of
   conscience in missions?
3. How does Paul's encounter with Peter in the second
   chapter of Galatians illustrate the significance of conscience in the New Testament church?
4. Why did Quaker Mary Dyer return to Boston knowing
   that she would be executed? What led her to take the
   risk?
5. Is it correct to consider the civil rights activities of
   African-American Christians a part of the church's mission in the world?
6. What expressions of conscience are evident in the
   church's mission today? Would we know them if we saw
   them?

The Unexpected: Risk and Irony

"Push, Sarah," the midwife said. Sarah pushed, and in an instant the child entered the world. "It's a boy, Sarah," one of the women cried, "it's a boy. And he looks just like you: wrinkled and toothless, wrinkled and toothless!" Sarah heard the baby's first cry and her weary old body shook with laughter.

Sometimes you just have to laugh. Life takes off in an unexpected, even unbelievable, direction, so unpredictable, so ironic, you just have to laugh. Sarah did, and the rest of us with her, perhaps. Remember Sarah? The above story is not in the biblical text, but reading that text you can almost imagine what might have been.

The word of God came to Sarah and her husband, Abraham, in the springtime of their lives. God promised that they would be parents of a great people, as numerous as the sands of the seashore. On one occasion God even "took Abram outside, and said, 'Look up into the sky, and count the stars if you can. So many,' he said, 'shall your descendants be' " (Gen. 15:5 NEB). But, mathematically speaking, before you can have multitudes, you must first have one, and at that Sarah and Abraham were not so lucky. Time passed, and "Abram's wife Sarai had borne him no children" (Gen. 16:1 NEB).

It looked as if Sarah's biological clock had stopped.

The situation got complicated when the frustrated couple secured a surrogate mother, the slave girl, Hagar, to give Abraham a son. According to custom, Sarah was to raise the child as her own and the appropriate genetic line was secured. Things did not work out smoothly, however. Hagar ran away, taking her child Ishmael, with her. The frustration continued.

Then one day when Sarah and Abraham were dwelling in a place called Mamre, three strangers showed up in the camp. Abraham extended desert hospitality to them, in the course of which one of the guests told them that by the same time next year, "Sarah your wife shall have a son" (Gen. 18:10*b* NEB). And Sarah, listening through the tent flap, heard the prediction and laughed her head off. The biblical text fairly giggles with Sarah's words: "I am past bearing children now that I am out of my time, and my husband is old" (Gen. 18: 12 NEB). As the text tells it, the "stranger" is actually "the Lord" in disguise and He took offense at Sarah's laughter. Actually, the story turns into a kind of comic interchange in which the stranger asked, "Why did Sarah laugh?" and then gives a one sentence sermon: "Is anything impossible for the Lord?" (Gen. 10:14 NEB). Sarah, on the other hand, got scared and in a bit of panic lied to the Lord, insisting that she did not laugh. And the story ends with the stranger's rejoinder to Sarah: "Yes, you did laugh!" And she did, didn't she? In fact, Sarah's situation reminds us that sometimes on the journey you just have to laugh. Life, even spiritual life, is filled with irony and the unexpected, and sometimes all you can do is laugh.

Did she laugh throughout the next nine months, wondering which hurt most, the rheumatism or the morning sickness? Did laughter, or at least a few chuckles, sustain her until the child, Isaac, whose name meant (what else?) *laughter,* was born? And Sarah summed it all up brilliantly when she said, "God has given me good reason to laugh, and everybody who hears will laugh with me" (Gen. 21:6 NEB).

Such laughter was apparently quite contagious, since Scripture says that Abraham laughed till he fell on his face (Gen. 17:17) when he heard the announcement. And we do laugh with them, don't we, half laughing at ourselves? We laugh because we, like Sarah, have known those moments when life got beyond us and all we could do was laugh, whether in joy, surprise, humiliation, or even despair.

Life and missions are full of ironies. It is hilarious, isn't it? After all those years of failure and frustration, after all the promises, now God tells us. It is like a bad joke, an unbelievable reality, an incomprehensible miracle, a blessed hope, and all you can do is laugh. Life is full of such moments. A kid goes out to fight a giant with nothing but a slingshot. Some people march around a military fortification blowing trumpets and the walls fall down. A woman refuses to move to the back of a segregated bus, like that would change anything in Montgomery, Alabama. A carpenter from Nazareth (can anything good come out of Nazareth?) shows up along the Sea of Galilee and some that fishermen believe He is the Christ of God. Or did some early Christians laugh cynically when somebody told them that Saul, the persecutor of Christians, had become one of them?

Sometimes you just have to laugh, perhaps because you are confused, scared, surprised, worried, or overwhelmed with joy. Sarah laughs when she hears that she is going to have a baby years after she had given up hope. You can almost hear her cackle: "Sure, I'm going to have a baby! And medicare will have to pay for it!" There is an understandable brittleness to her laughter; she had waited too long for the promises to be fulfilled.

But such brittleness does not last. Perhaps without knowing it, such laughter is one of the many stages of faith and missions. It is one of the risks we take when we are audacious enough to begin and continue on the journey of faith. Who knows where it will take us? Who knows what the results will be? To risk the journey is to open the door to the ironic, indeed, the hilarious side of missions. Sometimes in the missionary journey, you just have to laugh.

Nowhere is that more evident than in the stories from the American frontier. Missionaries, circuit riders and farmer-preachers had to learn to deal with the ironic, the humorous, and the downright irreverent if they were to communicate the gospel in that rough and tumble region of America. For example, they could not take for granted basic understanding of Christian history, beliefs, or knowledge of the Scriptures. One nineteenth-century circuit rider told of his travels deep into the American wilderness of Kentucky and Tennessee. He encountered a boy and began to inquire into his knowledge of Bible history. "Who killed Abel?" the preacher asked.

"I didn't know he was dead," the boy replied, "we just moved here last week."[1]

Methodist circuit rider Freeborn Garrettson reported of his frontier travels in the 1770s an occasion in which he asked a man, "Do you know Jesus Christ?"

"Sir," said the man, "I do not know where the gentleman lives." Thinking he was misunderstood, Garrettson repeated the question.

"I do not know him," the man again stated, "he must not live in these parts."[2]

A nineteenth-century Presbyterian missionary reached a remote cabin and asked the female inhabitant, "Are there any Presbyterians in this country?"

Supposing that the man was a frontier hunter, the woman replied: "Wal, I just couldn't say for sure about that. These woods is full of most every kind of varmet, but I ain't paid much attention to them. You might take a look around there on the back side of the cabin where my husband keeps his varmet hides, and see if he's got any Presbyterian hides nailed up. If there's any Presbyterians in this country, he's bound to have caught one by now."[3]

Bibles were scarce on the American frontier. One missionary-preacher related his attempts to sell a Bible to a frontier mother surrounded by her "brood" of children. He asked if the family had a Bible of their own and was told that they did. He asked to see the Bible and a search was undertaken, ultimately producing only a few worn pages. The preacher insisted these few pages did not constitute a Bible. Of course it did, the woman declared, "But I had no idea we were so nearly out."[4]

Frontier missionaries and preachers often confronted the issue of ministerial education. In some places it was welcomed; in others it was not. Some preachers had formal educational training; others did not. One nineteenth-century journal tells of a frontier preacher conducting a revival meeting where a stranger showed up in attendance. Concerned about the visitor's soul, the preacher inquired, "My friend, are you a Christian?"

The man replied, "Sir, I am a theological professor."

"My Lord," said the preacher, "I wouldn't let a little thing like that keep me from coming to Christ . . . ."[5]

The Christian missionaries and preachers on the American frontier were a unique group of individuals. Some were formally educated, others informally, while others were "Spirit educated" in their efforts to proclaim the gospel. Some could read, others could not. Some quoted Bible verses from memory while some made up verses as they went along. One frontier sermon illustrates: "I am an unlarnt Hardshell Baptist preacher of whom you've no doubt hearn afore, and I now appear here to expound the scriptures and pint out the narrow way which leads from a vain world to the streets of Jaroosalem; and my tex' which I shall choose for the occasion is in the leds of the Bible, somewhar between Second Chronicills and the last chapter of Timothytitus; and when you find it, you'll find it in these words: 'And they shall gnaw a file, and flee unto the mountains of Hepsidam, whar the lion roareth and the wang-doodle mourneth for his first-born."[6]

Perhaps no one personified the frontier mission more than the Methodist circuit rider Peter Cartwright. Cartwright was an outspoken missionary preacher who did not fear to confront his critics be they Baptists or infidels. His quick wit and directness were invaluable assets for adapting to frontier life. Some of the classic stories and rejoinders from frontier religion come from the mouth of Peter Cartwright.

In his autobiography, Cartwright described the great revival that swept the western frontier—Kentucky, Indiana, and Illinois—in the early nineteenth century. He wrote that, "In this revival, usually termed in the West the Cumberland revival, many joined the different Churches, especially the Methodist and Cumberland Presbyterians. The Baptists also came in for a share of the converts, but not to any great extent. Infidelity quailed before the mighty power of God, which was displayed among the people. . . . The Predestinarians [Presbyterians] of almost all sorts put forth a mighty effort to stop the work of God."[7] As a Methodist and committed to the workings of human free will, Cartwright had little patience with the predestinarian views of the Presbyterians and other adherents of Calvinism.

During these revivals, emotional outbursts were common to those under conviction of sin and searching for salvation. One of the most infamous outbursts took the form of the jerks, a phenomenon in which the entire body would convulse in violent shaking or jerking motions. Persons of all economic and social states fell under the power of the "exercises," as they were called. Cartwright tells of one occasion in which two sisters of upper-class family were seized by the jerks. Their brothers, horrified by the event, threatened to horsewhip Cartwright "for giving their sisters the jerks." In a moment of quick thinking, Cartwright advanced toward the brother who was threatening him and said , " 'Yes; if I gave your sisters the jerks I'll give them to you.' In a moment I saw he was scared. I moved toward him, he backed, I advanced, and he wheeled and ran, warning me not to come near him, or he would kill me. It raised the laugh on him, and I escaped my whipping. I had the pleasure before the year was out, of seeing all four [brothers and sisters] soundly converted to God, and I took them into the Church."[8]

Cartwright was also a master at using humor to distinguish himself and his beloved Methodism from the other denominations competing for members and orthodoxy on the frontier. He often debated Baptists over infant baptism, a practice he was more than willing (and able) to defend. On one occasion, when debating the baptism question, Cartwright set forth this argument. First, he noted that since Baptists did not baptize infants or children, then no children were members of Baptist churches. Second, even adults had to become like little children to receive baptism. Then, he wrote: "Finally, I proposed this question: 'Is not that Church which has no children in it more like hell than heaven?' I then added, 'If all hell was searched, there would not be a single child found in it; but all children are in heaven; therefore, there being no children in the Baptist Church, it was more like hell than heaven.' "[9]

Cartwright also knew how to use humor and irony in response to those whose religion got a bit out of hand. He recalls the occasion when a gentlemen claimed a divine revelation that Cartwright "was never to die, but to live forever." Cartwright continues: " 'Well,' said I, 'who revealed that to you?' He said, 'An angel.'
'Did you see him?' I asked.
'O yes,' was the reply; 'he was a white, beautiful, shining being.'
'Well,' said I, 'did you smell him?' This stumped him, and he said he did not understand me. 'Well,' said I, 'did the angel you saw smell of brimstone?' He paused, and I added, 'He must have smelled of brimstone, for he was from a region that burns with fire and brimstone, and consequently from hell; for he revealed a great lie to you, if he told you I was to live forever!' At this he slipped off, and never gave me any more trouble during the [revival] meeting.' "[10] Peter Cartwright preached the gospel on the frontier and used his quick wit to respond to the "wide open" religion of the day, revelations and all!

Irony was a necessity for many women who gave themselves to particular missions work. Sojourner Truth (1797?-1883), was an African-American abolitionist who traveled throughout the North calling for freedom for all black people. A former slave herself, Sojourner Truth often confronted hostile crowds who challenged her right to speak, both as a black and as a woman. On one occasion she was accosted by a man who declared: "Old woman, do you think your talk about slavery does any good? Do you suppose people care what you say? Why, I don't care any more for your talk than I do for the bite of a flea."

"Perhaps not," Sojourner replied, "but the Lord willing, I'll keep you scratching."[11]

When clergymen questioned her right to speak to men, she was quick with a response. "Some say woman can't have as much rights as a man cause Christ wasn't a woman. Where did Christ come from? From God and a woman. Man had nothing to do with him. If the first woman God ever made was strong enough to turn the world upside down all alone,

all women together ought to be able to turn it back and get
it right side up again and not what they are asking to do it,
the men better let 'em."[12]

Once, on a segregated railroad car, she occupied the whites
only section with a white woman companion. The conductor
tried to have her thrown off the train. When her friend protested
the conductor asked, "Does she belong to you?"

"She belongs to humanity," Sojourner's friend replied. The
conductor threw them both off the train. Sojourner Truth sued
the railroad for assault and battery and won. When it was over
she concluded that Northern railroad cars looked like "salt and
pepper" from then on.[13] Again, irony helped her confront bigotry, opening the door of freedom and equality for others.

Other women used irony to challenge young people to
accept the call to missions. In an editorial published in 1854,
Amelia Bloomer, an outspoken advocate of social reform and
charitable activity urged middle-class females to turn from idleness to activism. She wrote that, "Parents do a great injustice to
their daughters when they doom them to a life of idleness, or
what is worse, to a life of frivolity and fashionable dissipation.
It was said by a distinguished clergyman of one who has passed
away from earth. 'She ate, she drank, she slept, she dressed, she
danced and she died.' Such may be truly said to be the history
of many women of the present day. They eat, they drink, they
sleep, they dress, they dance and at last they die, without having accomplished the great purposes of their creation. Can
woman be content with this aimless, frivolous life? Is she satisfied to lead a mere butterfly existence, to stifle and crush all
aspirations for a nobler destiny, to dwarf the intellect . . . and
desecrate all the faculties which the Almighty Father has given
her and which He requires her to put to good use and give an
account thereof to him?"[14]

Irony also came in handy as a way of getting the attention
of folks in the pew in behalf of the missions enterprise. No one
in the 20th century was more committed to missions and its significance to the church than Nannie Helen Burroughs, one of
the most prominent female leaders among African-American
Baptists. Burroughs (1900-1961) was a founder of the Associ-

ation for the Study of Negro Life and History, as well as the first president of the National Training School for Women and Girls in Washington, D.C. For a time she was Corresponding Secretary for the Woman's Convention, Auxiliary to the National Baptist Convention. In that capacity she helped organized a national Woman's Day in African-American Baptist churches. The observance was to encourage women to participate in the effort to raise money and volunteers for missions and other benevolent causes. She was careful to remind Baptists that the day began primarily to "raise women," not money.[15]

Burroughs did not hesitate to use humor and irony to awaken her constituency. She even wrote a play that offered a humorous parody of the typical Baptist convention meeting from the welcome to the annual sermon to an "appeal for the redemption of Slabtown," a mythical community where the "Tenth Annual Session of the Women's District Convention" is being held.

The speaker's welcoming speech has a bit of an edge to it. "Times got so hard about a month ago, we started to write to you not to come, but our pastor told us to let you come on. People who are used to hard times at home need not expect better things away from home, especially if they ain't payin' for it. Some of the sisters are kinder complaining now. They say that women are big eaters and are more trouble than the men. . . . So you are welcome— thrice welcome. . . ."[16]

Responding to the welcome, one of the guests states: "I accept your welcome, such as it is. We shall hurry up and get through with our business and go home where we can get something to eat. We are sorry you are having such hard times here. Anybody who lived through the drought and the depression certainly can feed and sleep this handful of folks a few days. Of course, you all invited us . . . But we shall do the best we can and leave as soon as we can."[17]

The President's address begins: "Fellow officers, delegates, ladies and gentlemen . . . . I have traveled all over Slabtown visiting missionary societies and waking up sleepy leaders. . . . I have gone to a number of missionary societies where there is about as much spiritual life as you would find

in a graveyard. . . . Some of you missionary sisters are raising
money for missions and paying church debts and making presents to yourselves and your pastors. The Bible asks, 'Will a
man rob God?' I answer, yes. A man will not only rob God, but
he will get the women to help him. Sisters, it is not right for you
to raise money for missions and use it to make presents and pay
church debts."[18]

One observer noted: "Everybody Laughs the Evening
Through at Slabtown But Everybody Gets the Point." So
Burroughs helped groups of Baptists to laugh at themselves,
while calling attention to the needs of the world and the calling
of Christians to respond. In the "Appeal," Mrs. Betsy Lizzard sets
forth the standard. "We want people who'll 'sociate with us;
show us how to live; how to organize our community work;
build up our Sunday schools and missionary societies. Some
of them comes to church late, dressed like a lot of peacocks,
and sits back and look in pity or scorn on us make mistakes.
. . . There are just a few real ones. . . . We want teachers with
souls, heads and hands dedicated to the redemption of
Slabtown. They are in the world and we must find 'um."[19] So
humor informed the superficial piety and the need for genuine
servants within the body of Christ. Nannie Helen Burroughs
did her work well.

As we have noted earlier, risking the journey toward missions often means struggling with a new language and new customs in unfamiliar cultures. Few missionaries have escaped the
terrible and often humorous experiences of saying the wrong
thing at the wrong time in somebody else's language. When we
lived in Japan there was an occasion when an American missionary asked a Japanese Christian to give his "testimony"
recounting his conversion and Christian experience at the worship service on the following Sunday. The missionary mistak-
enly used the Japanese word for candy instead of testimony.
Next Sunday the would-be testifier appeared at church with
candy for everyone!

During the year I spent teaching in Fukuoka, Japan, I
worked hard to learn a bit of Japanese. With the help of a tape,
I memorized certain conversational phrases. One day, convers-

ing with a new Japanese friend, I used a Japanese phrase which I thought meant, "I have enjoyed our conversation." A missionary standing nearby told me later that what I said was better translated, "This conversation bores me." I hope I did not set Japanese Christianity too far back!

What does irony, humor, and sometimes downright craziness mean to the gospel task? Perhaps it is this: The gospel of Jesus Christ is serious business, involving matters of faith and hope, life and death, good and evil. Yet while we take the gospel very seriously, we do not always take ourselves seriously. We are, as Paul tell us, "earthen vessels," (2 Cor. 4:7) given to a variety of missteps and malapropisms, intentional and unintentional, in our efforts to carry the gospel to the world. To risk the journey is to risk the ironic. Sometimes the ironic is a way of sustaining us when the journey itself is long and hard, and we are not so sure about the way we are traveling.

So on our journeys let us laugh a little from time to time with Sarah and the angels, over all the folks who seemed far away from new life and sweet dreams who by grace seem to stumble into the kingdom of God. Or all the people on a thousand mission fields across two thousand years who were struck with unbearable sorrow and laughed through tears because if they had not laughed they just might have gone crazy. To laugh as Sarah and others did is to come to terms with the ironic side of life and faith, a way of coping with both joy and sorrow.

In October, 1993, my friend John Loftis and his fourteen-year-old daughter, Jessica, were killed in an automobile accident in Birmingham, Alabama. John was my student, friend, and colleague for almost 20 years. At their funeral we sang hymns of faith, cried together, and together recounted stories about John, some of which made us laugh. We would cry a little, and laugh a little, and cry some more. It was the only way to bear the sorrow of it all. And amid the tears and laughter we found God's presence together.

Frederick Buechner says, "that's what Jesus means when he stands in that crowd of cripples and loners and odd-balls and factory rejects and says, 'Blessed are you that weep now, for you shall laugh' " (Luke 6:21 RSV).[20] Isn't that what Sarah did when she heard that one so old was going to bear new life after all? You see, Sarah's story is not that far from our own. Grace doesn't always come as we think it should or fit neatly into our plans or involve the proper people or the proper occasions. Sometimes the solid rock of faith is built on the ironic, the unanticipated, and the surprising. Faith flabbergasts us and the laughter of cynicism turns to the laughter of celebration.

How can we be so sure? Because we, with the rest of the church, can read Isaiah's ancient words with eyes of faith that point us toward Jesus and the cross: "He grew up before the Lord like a young plant whose roots are in parched ground; he had no beauty, no majesty to draw our eyes, no grace to make us delight in him; his form, disfigured, lost all the likeness of a man, his beauty changed beyond human semblance. He was despised, he shrank from the sight of men, tormented and humbled by suffering; we despised him, we held him of no account, a thing from which men turn away their eyes. Yet on himself he bore our sufferings, our torments he endured, while we counted him smitten by God, struck down by disease and misery; but he was pierced for our transgressions, tortured for our iniquities; the chastisement he bore is health for us and by his scourging we are healed" (Isa. 53:1-5 NEB). Sort of makes you want to weep, doesn't it? Or laugh, out loud, for joy!

For Discussion

1. What evidences of irony do you find in the Old Testament? Suggest at least three.
2. What evidences of irony do you find in the New Testament? Suggest at least three.
3. How does humor affect the mission of the Christian church?
4. Was Nannie Helen Burroughs being irreverent in her drama about "Slabtown"? What was she attempting to communicate?
5. What experiences of humor or irony shape your response to the gospel?

The Risk of the Spirit

It all started with prayer, at least so it seemed. The formation of the first international missionary agency began with a prayer meeting. The idea was born in the now famous "Haystack Prayer meeting" held at Williams College, Williamstown, Massachusetts, at the beginning of the nineteenth century. It seems a group of college students, among them Samuel J. Mills, James Richards, Francis Robbins, Harvey Loomis, Gordon Hall, Luther Rice, and Byron Green were caught in a rainstorm while gathering for prayer. They sought refuge under a large haystack, prayed, experienced God's presence, and the rest is history. From their missionary calling and their sense of Divine direction came the American Board of Commissioners for Foreign Missions, founded in 1810 by American Congregationalists. This was the first such agency in the United States, and the organization which initially sent out Luther Rice and Ann and Adoniram Judson. It began, at least in part, as a result of prayer and a new sense of the Holy Spirit evident in the formation of new missionary organizations.[1]

Clearly, prayer and the life of the Spirit are central to the journey of the Christian. The church's missionary calling is intricately related to the spiritual life. Spirituality, the life of

113

God in the lives of men and women, is a popular term in contemporary culture. Today, many individuals seek spirituality in Bible study/prayer groups, in meditation on God's Word, and in contemplation of the Divine presence. These days, innumerable books point the individual to a variety of methods for cultivating the inner life of the Spirit. Some of these books represent the heritage of spirituality in the history of the Christian church. These "classics of Christian devotion" include writings from some of the church's great leaders. They include the *Confessions of St. Augustine*; the *Little Flowers of St.Francis*; various writings of St. Teresa of Avila and St. John of the Cross, medieval Spanish Christian mystics; the sermons of John Wesley; the journal of George Fox, the founder of the Quakers; and proponents of and participants in the spiritual life.

Some contemporary works reflect the impact of a kind of "pop" spirituality, which point the individual to certain styles for cultivating spirituality. Some of these "self-help" methods may be more helpful than others. It can get confusing. Indeed, not all approaches to spirituality are distinctively Christian.

Yet simply because others are pursuing the spiritual life in various forms, Christians should not neglect the way of spirituality nor ignore the classics of Christian devotion, nor hesitate to give themselves to meditation and reflection. The church has pursued the spiritual life since the first Christians came together for worship as described in the book of Acts: "With one mind they kept up their daily attendance at the temple, and, breaking bread in private houses, shared their meals with unaffected joy, as they praised God and enjoyed the favour of the whole people. And day by day the Lord added to their number those whom he was saving" (Acts 2:46 NEB).

Not long ago a friend of mine (who happens to be a Benedictine monk) visited the campus of Samford University in Birmingham, Alabama (where I teach). He lectured on the classics of Christian devotion and the role of monastic life in cultivating spirituality within the Christian tradition. He spoke of meditation, contemplation, prayer, and reflection as essential to the life of the Spirit. When he finished, a student, no doubt influenced by the impact of "pop" spirituality, inquired: "Aren't meditation, contemplation, and reflection evidences of the 'New Age' movement?"

"Oh, no," the monk replied, "for us it's 'Old Age.' We Benedictines have been praying and meditating since the fifth century!" For the Christian, therefore, spirituality is imperative. It is an absolute necessity for those who would make the journey toward the kingdom of God.

If it is so important, what then, is spirituality? How should it be defined? As we have noted, there are many definitions of spirituality, some distinctively Christian, others less so. For our purposes, spirituality might be defined as follows.

In short, spirituality involves the life of God in the lives of the people of God. It involves the cultivation of a continuing relationship with God. As earlier Christians saw it, spirituality was simply "the practice of the presence of God." It includes prayer, the study of the Scriptures, meditation on the truths of God's Word, worship, and personal reflection. Yet a life of and in the Spirit is not always simple. Because life itself is harsh, because human beings are sinners, and because Christians themselves are "earthen vessels" given to frailty and brokenness, the practice of God's presence can get very complicated very quickly. In that sense, spirituality is itself a risk. Like all human experiences it involves vulnerability, openness, and the possibility of danger. When persons open their hearts to the movement and leadership of the Spirit of God, they take a chance that hardship, hurt, and unpredictability may invade their lives.

Remember the nameless father who brought his epileptic son to Jesus and asked for healing? He was obviously at his wit's end, having sought help at every turn, all to no avail. He even implored the disciples to bring about healing. They tried and failed, and the man was again disappointed. Yet he tries one more time, imploring Jesus to do something. His response to Jesus is at the heart of the risk of the Spirit: " 'Lord, I have faith, help me where faith falls short' " (Mark

9:24 NEB). The father chooses to hold on to faith, hoping against hope that Jesus can do what all the others could not—provide some wholeness for his broken son. But his experience of life, his previous struggles and disappointments keep him from making the easy generalization or the glib confession. He believes and hopes, even amid his doubt. He casts his hopes on Christ, acknowledging the difficulty of it all. To follow Christ and cultivate life in the Spirit is to live by faith, confessing our uncertainties to the God who knows us as we are.

Nowhere is this element of the spiritual life more evident than in the missionary calling of the people of God. Consider the paradox of the spiritual life. On one hand it is prayer, study, and openness to the Spirit which sends us out to respond to the hurt and lostness of the world. Yet such a calling, such a response to the Divine mandate, compels us to be even more dependent on God's presence. The missionaries who served others in Christ's name at home and abroad, whether sent out by specific organizations or acting on their own, almost unknown to anyone else but God, confronted moments when the only sustaining power they could muster came from God alone.

To read the journals, letters, and other accounts of persons who acted in response to God's call is to discover the importance of prayer. It is also evidence of the way in which prayer and the presence of God sustained the people of God when the journey was difficult and the way was less than clear.

At times, prayer and the presence of God were all that stood between the missionaries and oblivion. When results were slow in coming or numerically negligible, the missionaries were forced to rely on their sense of call and their hope that God would indeed fulfill the mission entrusted to them.

More often than not, the early missionaries of the eighteenth and nineteenth centuries received only limited numerical response to their calls to Christian discipleship. They knew that they were planting seeds, but it the lack of clear-cut numerical success was clearly a frustration which troubled them. Frontier Texas preacher and missionary Z. N. Morrell illustrates the disappointments of missions and the sustaining power of prayer. In 1844 he was physically worn down and his wife was in declining health. He wrote: "My way was by no means clear. The church I first organized at Washington failed, and now the frontier church at Gonzales [was] scattered; my farming and financial operations all had failed, and in the midst of my distresses, like Jacob, after the loss of Joseph and Simeon, and the demand for Benjamin also, I could but cry out, 'All these things are against me;' and faith revealed no reason why these things should fail to 'bringdown my gray hairs with sorrow to the grave.' "[2]

In the midst of his difficulty, however, Morrell found strength in the struggles of the heroes of Biblical faith. He wrote: "The waters had not overflowed me, and the fires had not consumed me, and with a heart full of gratitude to Him who walked in the presence of Nebuchadnezzar with Shadrach, Meshach, and Abednego, in the midst of the fiery furnace, and who, walking upon the water Himself, caught the hand of the sinking Peter and restored him to his place, I buckled my armor on, and, with a fixed determination to fight his battles while I lived, went forth in what I supposed to be the line of duty."[3] Morrell found strength from the stories of those Biblical heroes who persevered when the way was rough. His own spiritual sense of the presence of God in his work also sustained him when the message was not received immediately.

William Carey (1761-1834), one of the chief architects of the modern mission movement, also knew those moments of despair and frustration. He, like others, turned to God's inescapable presence for strength. Ready to begin his work, Carey instead found himself stuck on shipboard, unable to travel because of war between France and England. Distressed by long delays for his trip to India and the beginning of a mission there, Carey wrote to his wife in 1793: "My stay here was very painful and unpleasant, but now I see the goodness of God in it. It was that I might hear the most pleasing accounts that I possibly could hear respecting earthly things. You wish to know in what state my mind is. I answer, it is much as when I left you. If I had all the world, I would freely give it all to have you and my dear children with me, but the sense of duty is so strong as to overpower all other considerations; I could not turn back without guilt on my soul. I find a longing to enjoy more of God; but, now I am among people of the world I think I see more beauties in godliness than ever, and, I hope, enjoy God more in retirement than I have done for sometime past."[4]

This quest for closer relationship with God amid the hardships of the missionary journey did not cease when Carey finally reached his destination. Indeed, it increased. In his recent biography of Carey, entitled *Faithful Witness*, Timothy George observes that, "Carey continued to struggle in prayer and search the Scriptures for that enjoyment of God which he found so elusive yet so alluring. He bemoaned his lack of [spiritual] progress. 'I think my peevishness, fretfulness, and impatience is astonishing. O that the grace of God might but be in me, and abound.' "[5]

In 1794 his 5-year-old son, Peter, died, and his wife, Dorothy, was gripped by a severe emotional and mental disturbance from which she would never recover. In despair, Carey wrote in his journal: "This is indeed the valley of the shadow of death to me, except that my soul is much more insensible than John Bunyan's Pilgrim. O what would I give for a kind sympathetic friend, such as I had in England, to whom I might open my heart! But I rejoice that I am here, notwithstanding; and God is here, who not only can have compassion, but is able to save to the uttermost."[6] When spiritual traumas took their toll, William Carey continued to risk his life on faith that God was indeed present with him.

We often overlook or forget the fact that the Bible, Old and New Testaments, much to say about prayer, decisions, petitions, praise, sorrows, struggles, indeed, all the crises and joys of life, is related to prayer in some way or another. Jesus Himself seemed to make prayer a part of almost every segment of His life. Thus we must recognize that if prayer is to be important and intricate to our own lives, it must be related to all of life. We cannot store it in a convenient box of religious things, using it only on identifiably religious occasions. Rather, prayer is part of all aspects of life. Sometimes prayer comes at specified, defined moments when we make a decided effort to experience God's presence. This is prayer as discipline—specific occasions when we intentionally reach out to God. Some spend lengthy periods each day in prayer to God. At such times they cultivate God's presence through the classic stages of prayer. These usually include various forms of adoration, confession, and intercession. Others, whose schedules or life rhythms may vary, are not able to sustain lengthy prayertimes, so they pray in shorter segments extended through out the day. Still others combine elements of both approaches.

My monastic friends have helped me understand the practice of prayer in new ways. They suggest that human beings cannot focus intense attention on anything, even God, for long periods of time. Thus, while they do not discourage lengthy prayertimes, in their common monastic life they shape their entire day around communion with God. Each day is divided into numerous segments from early morning to day's end. These brief experiences of prayer revolve around the reading or singing of the Psalms and prayerful intercession for the needs of the church and the world. They also believe that they can better focus their entire beings on God for short periods of time when they offer themselves entirely to God. In our increasingly busy lives we may find these monastic hints very helpful. Because of the demands of work, family, calling, and personal ministry, we may not be able to set aside long periods for prayer and reflection. But perhaps we can practice the presence of God in increments celebrated throughout each day.

Another place to cultivate both public and private prayer is in worship. Through prayer, the worshiping congregation reaches out to God and to each other. In prayerful worship, the words of our mouths and the meditations of our hearts are shared together in the presence of God. Those who pray audibly in worship articulate the hopes and concerns of the entire congregation.

Years ago in a variety of interim pastorates I began to write out my pastoral prayers for use in worship. I did so as a way of focusing my own thoughts and those of the congregation in specific directions around specific needs. On Saturday nights I would find time to pray and write. I tried to write the prayer, not as a speech or another sermon, but as conversation with God with and for other people. Strangely enough, I discovered that many persons responded to the prayers as often, if not more frequently than the sermons. It was a valuable lesson to learn.

Likewise, we should work hard to create moments of silence in each worship service. In silence, individuals may experience the presence of God through prayerful reflection and response. Silent prayer should not be considered "dead time" in the worship of God. Rather, it should allow for "space" in the worship service when persons can be still in God's presence, praying, listening, waiting, opening hearts and minds to the movement of the Spirit.

The New Testament church consistently came together for the exercise of prayer. In fact, it was in a prayer meeting that the Holy Spirit first came upon the church in power. The Holy Spirit exploded upon the church at Pentecost as they prayed together, and things have not been the same since.

Another experience of prayer may occur at what might be called the natural moment, a time not planned or even expected when we cry out to God in celebration, fear, or frustration. At these times words are less significant than the cry of the human spirit reaching out for God. This is prayer as the Psalmist described it: "Out of the depths have I cried unto thee, O Lord." (Psa 130:1 KJV). Its response is evident in Paul's superb reminder that, "In the same way the Spirit comes to the aid of our weakness. We do not even know how we ought to pray, but through inarticulate groans the Spirit himself is pleading for us, and God who searches our inmost being knows what the Spirit means, because he pleads for God's people in God's own way" (Rom. 8:26-28 NEB).

Prayer then is at once spoken and unspoken. It is a concentrated response to God and it is also a spontaneous cry for help in time of trouble and uncertainty. To pray is to believe that God hears and knows whatever the words, the circumstances, or the need. It is the audacious conviction that something happens to us, to others, even to God when we call out in faith. The story of Christian missions is the story of human beings crying "out of the depths" to God as they sought to respond to the call of the Gospel. Sometimes those cries are cries of assurance, sometimes of despair, they are always prayers of faith in the depths of human experience.

Only a brief survey illustrates the role of prayer in the missionary journey of faith. David Brainerd (1718-1747) was a young man who literally expended his life as a missionary to the Native Americans in the colonies. Afflicted with consumption, Brainerd nonetheless threw himself into the missionary task, facing hardships of frontier life and living in situations which only served to worsen his delicate condition. He died of consumption in the home of the renowned Puritan preacher, Jonathan Edwards. To honor Brainerd and extend his missionary vision, Edwards published the young man's journal. It became a popular source of missionary inspiration and Puritan spirituality for generations of evangelical Christians.

Brainerd's piety is couched in the self-effacing language of eighteenth-century Puritanism. His journal gives poignant indication of the depth of his prayers. "Lord's Day, April 4 [1742]. My heart was wandering and lifeless. In the evening God gave me faith in prayer, made my soul melt in some measure, and gave me to taste a divine sweetness. O my blessed God! Let me climb up near to Him, and love, and long, and plead, and wrestle, and stretch after Him, and for deliverance from the body of sin and death. Alas! my soul mourned to think I should ever lose sight of its Beloved again. 'O come, Lord Jesus, amen.' "[7]

Commenting on the spiritual state of the missionary, Jonathan Edwards observes in the edition of the journal: "On the evening of the next day, he complains that he seemed to be void of all relish of divine things, felt much of the preva-

lence of corruption, and saw in himself a disposition to all
[manner] of sin; which brought a very great gloom on his
mind and cast him down into the depths of melancholy.
. . ."⁸ Brainerd's approach to Christian spirituality is evident in
another journal entry, this one dated April 6, 1742: "Then I
cried to God to cleanse me from my exceeding filthiness, to
give me repentance and pardon. I then began to find it sweet
to pray; and could think of undergoing the greatest sufferings,
in the cause of Christ, with pleasure. . . . Then God gave me
to wrestle earnestly for others, for the kingdom of Christ in
the world, and for dear Christian friends. I felt weaned from
the world and from my own reputation amongst men, willing
to be despised and to be gazing stock for the world to
behold. It is impossible for me to express how I then felt."⁹

Brainerd's spirituality, his sense of the presence of God
and his own spiritual state, is expressed in the language of a
certain type of Puritan piety evident in the eighteenth century.
It reflects powerful struggles with sin and self. Brainerd and
other Puritans rejoiced in God's grace but could never escape
their sense of their own total depravity. While they believed
that God was present with them, they also struggled moment
by moment with what seemed their utter sinfulness which
ever kept them at odds with grace. Their language is filled
with references to their evil natures and the dark side of life.
Nonetheless, it also indicates the intensity of faith for these
individuals and the significance of prayer and spiritual reflection in their lives.

The "everydayness" of prayer is also evident in missionary
journals. Through out the journal of David Livingstone (1813-
1873) there are daily prayers and spiritual reflections offered
to God by the renowned Scottish missionary-explorer.
Livingstone was a preacher, physician, explorer and map-
maker who spent over 30 years as a missionary in Africa. It is
said that when he died in Africa in 1873, it was on his knees,
in the position of prayer. Journal entries include the following: "19th March. [1872]. Birthday prayer: My Jesus, my king,
my life, my all. Once more I dedicate my whole self to Thee.
Accept me and grant, O gracious Father, that ere this year is

gone, I may finish my task. In Jesus' name I ask it. Amen, so let it be. David Livingstone. 13th May [1872]. He will keep His work, the gracious One—full of grace and truth. He said: 'Him that cometh unto Me I shall in no wise cast out.' He *will* keep His word. Then I can come humbly and present my petition, and it will be all right. Doubt here is inadmissible, surely. D.L."[10]

"30 July [1872]. What is the atonement of Christ? It is Himself. It is the inherent and everlasting mercy of God made apparent to human eyes and ears. The everlasting love was disclosed by our Lord's life and death. It showed that God forgives because He loves to forgive. He works by smiles if possible; if not, by frowns. Pain is only a means of enforcing love. If we speak of strength, lo! He is strong. The Almighty. The Over Power. The Mind of the Universe. The heart thrills at the idea of His greatness."[11]

The spirituality of the early missionaries also sustained them when their message was not readily received by those to whom it was offered. In fact, most of the early Christian missionaries did not give evidence of what might be called a "significant convert ratio." More often than not, their efforts were not immediately welcomed. Yet they came to believe that they were planting seeds which someday, by God's grace, would bear fruit. They were correct, and many did not live to see the the results of their labor. Thus their faith in the power of the Gospel and their hope for the fulfillment of their vision sustained them. Theirs was a powerful witness, even to those who did not immediately respond.

Consider David Livingstone. As far as we know, he made only one known convert, a man named Sechele, who, it is said, later turned from the faith. Yet for ten months after his death in 1873, some sixty Africans carried the body of the beloved Livingstone from Lake Bangweolo to the African coast where it could be shipped back to England. Not one of those persons who carried the sun-dried, salt-preserved body claimed to be a Christian. Yet even in death the power and simplicity of Livingstone's spirituality was evident.[12] Today, Africa is a nation of millions of Christians. The seed blossomed, didn't it?

Robert Morrison (1782-1834) was the first Protestant missionary to China. He arrived in Canton in 1807 and it was not until 1814 that his first convert, Tsae A-Ko, was baptized. During the rest of his tenure in China, only ten additional converts were baptized. Yet Morrison continued, sustained no doubt by the spiritual life and the sense, even in times of discouragement, that God would give the increase.

The Baptist missionary Lottie Moon also knew those moments of discouragement when few people responded to her mission. One scholar wrote of her mission work in P'ingtu, a region of China where no Baptist missionary work had been done before: "A logical restructuring of events indicates that she had indeed miscalculated in P'ingtu at virtually every turn. Her leavening evoked no conversions in the city, and her austere life did not strike her neighbors as identical with their own."[13]

Nonetheless, "Sister Lottie" was concerned to provide a witness, continuing her spiritual devotion to God. She wrote: "The missionary's first object is to convince them [the Chinese] that he is human and that he is their sincere friend. By patience and gentleness and unwearied love, he wins upon them until there begins to be a diversion in sentiment."[14] When the way was rough, Lottie Moon turned to the fruits of the Spirit, gentleness, patience, and love (Gal. 5), as the foundation of her life and mission.

These accounts remind us that the work of the missionary is hard work. It involves great stress and not a little frustration. Thus the people of God must seek the presence of God in the celebration of spiritual victories and the bone-tired moments of spiritual and physical exhaustion. The journey of missions is the journey of prayer and contemplation. It is the recognition that God is present in all of life, its celebration and its sorrows. And if that is so, then prayer must be present in all of life as well. In prayer we can and must be brutally honest with God about ourselves, our friends, our enemies, our hurts, and our sins.

The life of the Spirit, therefore, is not found simply knowing God, although that is essential. It is also found in realizing that *God knows us* and is with us no matter where we are, what we have done, or what the circumstances may be. Martin Luther (1483-1546), the great Protestant reformer, experienced terrible periods of depression all his life. He called such times his *anfectungen*—despair—when he felt as if there was no hope and no way of escape from doubts and fears. At such times, Luther would remember his baptism, administered when he was but an infant. In baptism, Luther believed, it was not simply that he had chosen Christ but that Christ had chosen him. No matter how his own feelings and emotions might change, Christ was unchanging and He held Luther tightly in His loving, forgiving embrace.

So it is with us. We, too, can know that Christ has chosen us and clings to us even in the depths of despair. That assurance accompanies us on mission. It is the promise of the Spirit in the difficult places of life. It is the strength of God's good presence which we experience through prayer, Scripture, worship, and contemplation. It is good news for all those who risk the journey, answering God's call to proclaim His word!

FOR DISCUSSION

1. Define Christian spirituality as you understand it.
2. What is your response to the monastic idea of prayer as described in this chapter?
3. How did spirituality influence and sustain the missionaries cited here?
4. How would you interpret David Brainerd's approach to the spiritual life as described in this chapter?
5. When is spirituality risky?

NOTES

Chapter 1

1. Miron Winslow, *Memoir of Mrs. Harriet L. Winslow* (New York: Garland Publishing, Inc., 1987), 323-4.
2. Francis M. DuBose, ed., *Classics of Christian Missions* (Nashville: Broadman Press, 1979), 233.
3. S. M. Houghton, *Five Pioneer Missionaries* (London: Banner of Trust, 1965), 271.
4. Ibid., 31.
5. Ibid., 320.
6. Ibid., 341.
7. Roland H. Bainton, *Here I Stand* (Nashville: Abingdon-Cokesbury Press, 1950), 181.
8. Ibid., 182.

Chapter 2

1. Eduard Schweizer, *The Good News According to Matthew* (Atlanta: John Knox Press, 1974), 471.
2. Ibid., 472.
3. Ibid., 471.
4. Ibid., 472-3.
5. Ibid., 472.
6. DuBose, *Christian Missions*, 26.
7. William L. Andrews, *Sisters of the Spirit* (Bloomington: Indiana University Press, 1986), 141-2.
8. J. Stevenson, *A New Eusebius* (London: SPCK, 1970), 21.
9. Julian Pettifer and Richard Bradley, *Missionaries* (London: BBC Books, 1990), 23.
10. Ibid., 19.

Chapter 3

1. Martin E. Marty, Memo, *The Christian Century* vol. 109, no. 21

(July 1-8, 1992): 663.
2. H. Leon McBeth, *A Source Book for Baptist Heritage* (Nashville: Broadman Press, 1990), 207.
3. Ibid., 208.
4. Ibid., 206-207.
5. Ibid., 208.
6. Robert A. Baker, *The Blossoming Desert* (Waco, TX: Word, Inc., 1970) 43.
7. W. P. Strickland, *Autobiography of Peter Cartwright* (New York: Phillips and Hunt, 1856), 74-75.
8. Ibid., 80-81.
9. Ibid., 133-134.
10. Timothy George, *Faithful Witness: The Life and Mission of William Carey* (Birmingham: New Hope, 1991) 163.
11. Ibid., 163.

Chapter 4

1. Conrad Cherry, *God's New Israel* (Englewood Cliffs, NJ: Prentice-Hall, Inc., 1971), 31.
2. Ibid., 31.
3. Rosemary Radford Ruether and Rosemary Skinner Keller, *Women and Religion in America Volume 2: 1990-1968* (San Francisco: Harper and Row, 1981), 301-302.
4. Ibid., 301.
5. Edwin S. Gaustad, ed., *A Documentary History of Religion in America to the Civil War* (Grand Rapids, MI: William B. Eerdmans Publishing Company, 1982), 395, 396-7.
6. Ibid., 397, 399-400.
7. Bill J. Leonard, *Word of God Across the Ages* (Nashville: Broadman

Press, 1981), 79.
[8]Peggy Dow, *The Dealings of God, Man, and the Devil* (New York: Sheldon, Lamport, and Blakeman, 1956), 202.
[9]McBeth, *Baptist Heritage*, 225.
[10]Ibid., 225.
[11]Ibid., 225-6.
[12]Ibid., 226.
[13]Ibid., 163.
[14]Ibid., 163.
[15]Dow, *Dealings of God*, 207.

Chapter 5

[1]J. Stevenson, *New Eusebius*, 127.
[2]McBeth, *Baptist Heritage*, 204.
[3]Ibid., 205.
[4]Ibid., 215.
[5]William G. McLoughlin, *Cherokees and Missionaries, 1789-1839* (New Haven: Yale University Press, 1984), 155.
[6]Ibid., 155.
[7]Ibid., 155.
[8]Ibid., 156.
[9]Ibid., 156.
[10]Ibid., 157.
[11]Ibid., 160.
[12]Irwin T. Hyatt, Jr., *Our Ordered Lives Confess* (Cambridge, MA: Harvard University Press, 1976), 5-6.
[13]Ibid., 60.
[14]Ibid., 60.
[15]Leonard, *Word of God*, 81.
[16]Ibid., 81.

Chapter 6

[1]Carlyle Marney, *Priests to Each Other* (Greenville, SC: Smyth & Helwys Publishing, In., 1991).
[2]Stevenson, *Eusebius*, 12.
[3]Rufus Jones, *Studies in Mystical Religion* (n.p., n.d.).
[4]Nancy A. Hardesty, *Great Women of Faith* (New York: Baker Book House, 1980) 35.
[5]Ibid., 36.
[6]Robert Pierce Beaver, *American Protestant Women in World Mission* (Grand Rapids, MI: William B. Eerdmans Publishing Company, 1980) 14-5.
[7]McBeth, *Baptist Heritage*, 211.
[8]Hardesty, *Women of Faith*, 82.
[9]Ibid., 84.
[10]Ibid., 73.
[11]Ibid., 73.
[12]Ibid., 74.
[13]Ibid., 127.

Chapter 7

[1]DuBose, *Christian Missions*, 146-7.
[2]Ibid., 151.
[3]Ibid., 229-30.
[4]Ibid., 231.
[5]Ibid.,231.
[6]Ibid., 234.
[7]Ibid., 83.
[8]Winslow, *Memoir*, 67-8.
[9]Ibid., 68.
[10]Ibid., 69.
[11]Ibid., 353.
[12]Ibid., 437.
[13]Ibid., 439.
[14]Ibid., 462.
[15]Stephen Neill, *Christian Missions*, (Grand Rapids, MI: Eerdmans, 1965), 318-19.
[16]Albert Schweitzer, *On the Edge of the Primeval Forest* (London: A. & C. Black, Ltd., 1922), 1-2.
[17]Ibid., 176.
[18]Neill, *Christian Missions*, 317.

Chapter 8

[1]William Warren Sweet, *The Story Religion in America* (New York: Harper and Row, 1950), 69.
[2]Ibid., 69.
[3]Sidney E. Mead, *The Lively*

Experiment (New York: Harper and Row, 1963), 13.

⁴William Owen Carver, *Missions in the Plan of the Ages* (Nashville: Broadman, 1951), 198.

⁵Gaustad, *Religion in America*, 115.

⁶Ibid., 115-6.

⁷Ruether and Keller, *Women in Religion*, 281.

⁸Gaustad, *Religion in America*, 134-5.

⁹William G. McLouglin, *Soul Liberty* (Hanover, NH: University Press on New England), 183.

¹⁰Ibid., 186.

¹¹McLouglin, *Soul Liberty*, 196-201.

¹²Bill J. Leonard, *Early American Christianity* (Nashville: Broadman, 1983), 184-5.

¹³Sweet, *Religion and American Culture*, 329.

¹⁴Lerone Bennett, Jr., *Before the Mayflower: A History of the Negro in America 1619-1964* (Baltimore, MD: Viking-Penguin Books, 1988), 146.

¹⁵Reuther and Keller, *Women in Religion* vol. 1, 297.

¹⁶Ibid., 323.

¹⁷Ibid., 297.

¹⁸Ibid., 325.

¹⁹Ibid., 319.

Chapter 9

¹Ross Phares, *Bible in Pocket, Gun in Hand* (Lincoln: University of Nebraska Press, 1964), 1-2.

²Ibid., 1.

³Ibid., 4.

⁴Ibid., 5.

⁵Ibid., 13.

⁶T. Clark, *The Rampaging Frontier* (Bloomington: Indiana University Press, 1964), 157.

⁷Strickland, *Peter Cartwright*, 48.

⁸Ibid., 49-50.

⁹Ibid., 227-8.

¹⁰Ibid., 228-9.

¹¹Leonard, *Word of God*, 71.

¹²Ibid., 71.

¹³Ibid., 72.

¹⁴Reuther and Keller, *Women and Religion* vol. 1, 298.

¹⁵Ibid., 118-21.

¹⁶Ibid., 126.

¹⁷Ibid., 126.

¹⁸Ibid., 126.

¹⁹Reuther and Keller, *Women and Religion* vol. 3, 127.

²⁰Frederick Buechner, *Peculiar Treasures* (San Francisco: Harper and Row, 1979), 153.

Chapter 10

¹R. Glover, *The Progress of Worldwide Missions* (New York: Harper and Row, 1960), 61.

²Baker, *Blossoming Desert*, 63.

³Ibid., 63.

⁴George, *Faithful Witness*, 83.

⁵Ibid., 108.

⁶Ibid., 109.

⁷Leonard, *American Christianity*, 297.

⁸Ibid., 297-8.

⁹DuBose, *Christian Missions*, 194.

¹⁰Ibid., 197.

¹¹Pettifer and Bradley, *Missionaries*, 82.

¹²Leonard, *Word of God*, 84.

TEACHING GUIDE

Before the study:
- read the book, decide how you will teach it, and prepare any handouts, posters, etc.;
- encourage all participants to read the book;
- plan for publicity and promotion;
- enlist small group facilitators; communicate what their responsibilities will be within the small groups;
- prepare posters with these words: Missions, Faith, Identity, Place, Community, Ministry, Sacrifice, Conscience, Irony, Humor. Mount posters on walls around the room where the study will take place.
- have a supply of paper and pencils for use throughout the study. If study time is limited, select appropriate segments of the book which are to be taught.

Teaching Plan
This study is divided into five segments. After determining how much time you have for the study, read the teaching plan below, then decide how much time you will allow for each segment.

• Large Group
Begin the study with prayer and appropriate introductions. Explain the purpose of the book and the study, and give a brief overview of the activities that will follow.

Give each participant a piece of paper. Ask participants to write a one sentence definition of words on the posters. Allow time for participants to share their definitions and make comments. Ask those who have read the book if their definitions were affected by their reading of the book.

Conclude the large group time with a discussion of risk involved in the Christian journey.

• Small Groups

Divide the large group into smaller groups. Assign one or two chapters from the book to each of the groups, depending on the number of groups. Each small group will need a facilitator; this person needs to be familiar with the assigned chapter(s) and sensitive to the fact that some participants may not have read the book prior to the study.

Facilitators will use the questions at the end of each chapter and these questions to guide a discussion:

- What do the issues raised in these chapters suggest about the nature of the Christian journey?
- How do these issues inform the way your local congregation understands the church's mission?
- How do these issues relate to the risk involved in the Christian journey?

• Individual study

After the small group discussion, facilitators will instruct participants to work individually. Each participant will select one segment of the chapter studied and write a brief (one page) essay about a new insight or understanding gained during this study.

• Partners

After writing the essays, participants share and discuss what they wrote with a partner. Ask them to be prepared to briefly share their insights with the group.

• Large Group

All participants will gather again in the large group. Invite participants to discuss issues raised in small groups and through the individual essays.

Conclude with a discussion of the implications of these issues for the future of Christianity and the individual's Christian journey.

Close with a prayer for missionary work.

Church Study Course Credit

Church Study Course credit for this book may by received by group or individual study. Group study requires participation in a 2 ½ hour class study and personal study of the material not covered in class. If you choose to study it individually, read the entire book and complete all "For Discussion" questions. After completing the course, complete Form 725 and send it to the Awards Office, 127 Ninth Avenue, North, Nashville, TN 37324. Forms can be obtained from your church, association, or state office, or from the Baptist Sunday School Board Office. This book is course number 03-421 in the Church Study Course.